ILLUSTRATED

MINUTE

BIOGRAPHIES

LOUISA MAY ALCOTT • ALFRED THE GREAT • ALEXANDER THE GREAT
ATTILA THE HUN • HANS CHRISTIAN ANDERSEN • JOHN JAMES AUDUBON
ARISTOTLE • HONORE DE BALZAC • JOHANN SEBASTIAN BACH • CLARA BARTON
PHINEAS TAYLOR BARNUM • LUDWIG VAN BEETHOVEN • JOHANNES BRAHMS
ALEXANDER GRAHAM BELL • JOHN BROWN • DANIEL BOONE
LUTHER BURBANK • LORD BYRON • JULIUS CAESAR • ANDREW CARNEGIE
CATHERINE THE GREAT • KIT CARSON • ENRICO CARUSO • CASANOVA
WILLIAM CAXTON • FREDERIC FRANCOIS CHOPIN • BENVENUTO CELLINI
CHARLEMAGNE • WINSTON L. S. CHURCHILL • CLEOPATRA • CONFUCIUS
WILLIAM FREDERICK CODY • CHRISTOPHER COLUMBUS
JEAN BAPTISTE COROT • JAMES FENIMORE COOPER • MME. MARIE CURIE
CHARLES ROBERT DARWIN • DANTE • CHARLES DICKENS
FERDINAND DE SOTO • ALEXANDRE DUMAS • BENJAMIN DISRAELI
ANTON DVORAK • THOMAS ALVA EDISON • ALBERT EINSTEIN
DWIGHT D. EISENHOWER • ELIZABETH THE QUEEN • ERASMUS
RALPH WALDO EMERSON • MICHAEL FARADAY • HENRY FORD
BENJAMIN FRANKLIN • STEPHEN COLLINS FOSTER • ROBERT FULTON
FREDERICK THE GREAT • THOMAS GAINSBOROUGH • GALILEO • GANDHI
GEORGE GERSHWIN • JOHANN WOLFGANG VON GOETHE • ULYSSES S. GRANT
EDVARD GRIEG • VINCENT VAN GOGH • JOHANN GUTENBERG • NATHAN HALE
HANNIBAL • WILLIAM HARVEY • ALEXANDER HAMILTON • HENRY VIII
PATRICK HENRY • VICTOR HERBERT • HIPPOCRATES • WINSLOW HOMER
HOMER • JULIA WARD HOWE • HENRY HUDSON • VICTOR HUGO
ANDREW JACKSON • JESUS • THOMAS JEFFERSON • JOHN PAUL JONES
BEN JONSON • JOAN OF ARC • ROBERT KOCH • KUBLAI KHAN • LAFAYETTE
NIKOLAI LENIN • ROBERT E. LEE • ABRAHAM LINCOLN
HENRY WADSWORTH LONGFELLOW • MARTIN LUTHER
GEN. DOUGLAS MACARTHUR • MARCO POLO • MARY QUEEN OF SCOTS
JOHN MARSHALL • MICHELANGELO • MARK TWAIN • MARIE ANTOINETTE
MENDELSSOHN • MOHAMMED • MOSES • JAMES MONROE
WOLFGANG AMADEUS MOZART • NAPOLEON BONAPARTE • NERO
JOHN HENRY CARDINAL NEWMAN • SIR ISAAC NEWTON • FLORENCE NIGHTINGALE
EUGENE GLADSTONE O'NEILL • LOUIS PASTEUR • JOHN J. PERSHING
WILLIAM PENN • PABLO PICASSO • WILLIAM SIDNEY PORTER • PLATO
SIR WALTER RALEIGH • REMBRANDT • PAUL REVERE • AUGUSTE RODIN
FRANKLIN DELANO ROOSEVELT • THEODORE ROOSEVELT
WILHELM KONRAD VON ROENTGEN • GEORGE HERMAN RUTH
FRANZ PETER SCHUBERT • WILLIAM SHAKESPEARE • SOCRATES
GEORGE BERNARD SHAW • ROBERT LOUIS STEVENSON
HARRIET BEECHER STOWE • PETER ILYITCH TCHAIKOVSKY
ARTURO TOSCANINI • COUNT LEO TOLSTOY • HARRY S. TRUMAN
JULES VERNE • VOLTAIRE • LEONARDO DA VINCI • QUEEN VICTORIA
RICHARD WAGNER • GEORGE WASHINGTON • H. G. WELLS • DANIEL WEBSTER
NOAH WEBSTER • CHAIM WEIZMANN • ELI WHITNEY • WALT WHITMAN
ROGER WILLIAMS • WOODROW WILSON • SIR CHRISTOPHER WREN
WILBUR AND ORVILLE WRIGHT

ILLUSTRATED
MINUTE
BIOGRAPHIES

150 FASCINATING LIFE-STORIES OF FAMOUS PEOPLE
FROM THE DAWN OF CIVILIZATION TO THE PRESENT DAY
DRAMATIZED WITH PORTRAITS AND
SCENES FROM THEIR LIVES

Designed and Illustrated by
SAMUEL NISENSON

Text by
WILLIAM A. DeWITT

GROSSET & DUNLAP · *Publishers*

NEW YORK

To the Memory of
ALEXANDER GROSSET
*whose enthusiasm and encouragement
made it possible
this book is gratefully dedicated*

CONTENTS

IX

Author and Heroine
of "Little Women"
LOUISA MAY
ALCOTT

WHEN STILL A CHILD, Louisa May Alcott decided to make a great deal of money. Though her father, Amos Bronson Alcott, was a famous school teacher and philosopher, he had little practical sense. His visionary schemes always failed, and his wife and four daughters lived constantly in poverty. Hence Louisa May's desire for money, to bring comfort to her family. Hence, also her later definition of a philosopher: "A man up in a balloon, with his family and friends holding the ropes which confine him to earth and trying to haul him down."

Born at Germantown, Pa., Nov. 29, 1832, Louisa May started her money-making career as a dressmaker for dolls. Willing to do almost anything to further her ambition, she later taught school, sewed, and worked as a household servant. But always she wrote stories. At first she was lucky to earn five or ten dollars apiece for them. Then, in 1860, the *Atlantic Monthly* magazine paid her what seemed like a princely sum — fifty dollars — for a single story.

It was not until the Civil War, though, that she became really famous. For six weeks in the winter of 1862-63 she served as a nurse in the Union Army hospital Georgetown, D. C. In that short period the hard work and privation ruined her health for life. But from the experience she wrote a book called *Hospital Sketches*, which had a very wide sale and made her a celebrity.

Little Women, her next book, published in 1868, is the one for which she is still beloved by American girls. It was the most popular of all her books, and "Jo," its heroine, was of all her characters most like Louisa May herself. There were other popular books — *Jo's Boys, An Old-Fashioned Girl, Little Men* and *Moods,* to mention a few.

Louisa May Alcott also won fame for her generosity, giving both money and time to friends, relatives and strangers alike, and for her activity in behalf of such causes as women's suffrage and the abolition of slavery. From overwork and the long illness resulting from her service as a nurse during the Civil War, she died just two days after her father, on March 6, 1888.

ALFRED
THE GREAT

*Noblest
of
English Kings*

No ruler in history has so well deserved to have "the Great" used after his name as Alfred. Coming to the English throne in 871, at the age of twenty-three, he fought for twenty-five years to rid his land of the barbarian Danish invaders. It was a see-saw battle, with the Danes often leading, but in the end, by 896, Alfred thoroughly defeated them.

His victory saved not only England, but all of western Europe, from becoming part of a heathen Scandinavian empire, for the Danes had not yet learned Christianity. Alfred was a magnificent soldier, but his other accomplishments outshone his military deeds.

Besides leading the English armies, he reorganized them on a more efficient basis, and also began an increase of the navy that led finally to Britain's supremacy on the seas. He even designed ships himself.

After the disruption wrought by the Danes, Alfred had to reorganize the civil government. His success in this was great, and for his administration of justice he won the title, "protector of the poor." Under the Danes the Church, and particularly the monasteries, had suffered severely. Since education at that time was a special province of the Church, ignorance was widespread. Alfred founded two or three new monasteries, but did not actually revive the system of monasticism. What he did was to start a court school and import scholars for it.

Moreover, he studied hard himself. So that knowledge of Latin, considered the chief civilized language in the Middle Ages, again would become general among the clergy, he began writing a series of translations. In these books he sometimes wrote prefaces or added thoughts and information of his own. Thus, later scholars learned much about Alfred and his times.

One of these sentences has been often quoted to show what kind of a man Alfred was: "My will was to live worthily as long as I lived, and after my life to leave to them that should come after, my memory in good works." Alfred died in 900, more than a thousand years ago, but the memory of his good works still lives.

World Conqueror

ALEXANDER
THE GREAT

No soldier in history, including Napoleon, has to his credit the military accomplishments of Alexander, king of Macedon.

At the age of eighteen he won his first triumph, commanding cavalry that were the decisive factor at the Battle of Chaeronea, won by his father, Philip II. This was in 338 B.C. Two years later he ascended the throne of his tiny Greek state and quickly subdued a host of enemies in neighboring states. By 334 B.C. he was ready for the monumental task of attacking Persia, Greece's traditional enemy.

Starting in early spring with only 30,000 foot soldiers and 5,000 horse, he invaded Asia through what is now Turkey and by May had routed the Persian army on the banks of the river Granicus. Moving swiftly east, then south, he took the whole Syrian coast and thus destroyed Persia's sea power. Egypt submitted without a blow. Within the next seven years Alexander swept eastward across Persia and Baluchistan clear into India, winning three titanic battles and innumerable lesser engagements. In his decisive Assyrian victory at Arbela

the Persians opposing his meager forces were estimated to number a million men. But in 323 B.C., when all his preparations for the conquest of Arabia were made, Alexander fell ill of a fever and died, at the age of thirty-three.

In comparing him with Napoleon it is said that the latter's influence vanished before his death, whereas the marks of Hellenic culture spread by Alexander endured for centuries. One of his most remarkable policies was to encourage the fusion with the Greeks of conquered races. He himself married the daughter of Darius, Persian commander, as well as Roxana, the wife of his choice, and Parysatis, a third Asian princess.

A man of great physical courage, Alexander fought according to the custom of his times, in the front ranks, and more than once was wounded almost mortally. He had incredible energy, and tremendous personal charm. His only weakness was drinking: in a drunken brawl at Samarkand he killed his foster-brother, Clitus, and it was after two nights of banqueting that he caught his fatal fever.

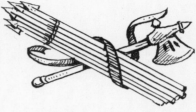

"The Scourge of God"

ATTILA
THE HUN

IT is one of the less-remembered ironies of history that this savage and ruthless marauder used as an excuse for some of his bloody raids on western Europe the daughter of a Byzantine Emperor—Honoria, whose father was Theodosius II. As a young woman Honoria came under discipline because of a love affair that was discovered. She sent her ring to Attila, begging him to be her rescuer and husband. Though he did nothing about it, Attila used his position as "fiancé" for a pretext to make outrageous demands. Once he even claimed half of Roman Emperor Valentinian III's domain as a dowry.

Attila became king of the Huns in 434, at first as co-ruler with his brother, Bleda. Insatiably ambitious, he soon reigned alone, possibly as a result of murdering his brother.

Through clever and energetic warfare, within eight years of his accession, Attila was in almost unopposed possession of Central Europe, with his capital near present-day Budapest. Looking for new fields to conquer, in the year 451 he led a barbarian army of three-quarters of a million men, including his allies, the Franks and the Vandals, across the Rhine to sack most of the cities of Belgic Gaul. He even laid siege to the city of Orleans and might have taken it but for the arrival of the Romano-Gothic army of Aëtius and Theodoric, king of the Visigoths.

The two armies met on the Catalaunian Fields in what was one of the decisive battles of history. Theodoric lost his life, but his army won the day—a bloody day indeed. Still, though Attila retreated, he retreated in good order, saving his forces, and the following year he made himself felt again in Christian Europe by laying waste much of northern Italy. Italian refugees, looking for shelter in the Adriatic lagoons, made the foundations of Venice. On this expedition Attila even threatened Rome, and it required a plea from Pope Leo I to send him back across the Alps. He died on the eve of a new Italian invasion, in 453.

Attila has had much attention in Teutonic legend under the name of Etzel and in Scandinavian Saga under the name of Atli.

[14]

Teller of Immortal Fairy Tales

HANS CHRISTIAN
ANDERSEN

Andersen's enchanting fairy stories won him world-wide renown. They were translated into nearly every European language, and are still a delight to millions of children and adults. But the author himself disdained them. The acclaim he really wanted was for his novels and plays, and this he never achieved.

Son of a shoemaker, Hans was born April 2, 1805, at Odense in Denmark. Signs of a remarkable imagination appeared when he was very young and his parents indulged his eccentric temperament to an unusual degree. He was only eleven when his father died, but from that time on he did exactly what he wanted. Going to school was not included.

The theater fascinated him then as always. He built a toy stage, made costumes for his puppets, and read all the plays he could lay hands on, among them those of Shakespeare. Then, at the age of fourteen, deciding to become an opera-singer, he calmly set off for Copenhagen.

There, on hearing his voice, theater managers pronounced him a lunatic to entertain ambitions to be a singer, but he did succeed in being taken into the Royal Theatre as a dancing pupil. Nothing much came of this venture, except that Hans won the attention of King Frederick VI, who sent him for several uncomfortable years to the grammar school at Slagelse.

His first writing success came in 1829, with a book called *A Journey on Foot from Holman's Canal to the East Point of Amager*. Later the King gave him a traveling allowance and he wrote other books about his long journeys through Europe. The earliest instalment of *Fairy Tales* appeared in 1835, but excited him much less than a novel called *The Improvisatore*, which was published the same year. Readers in the beginning shared Andersen's opinion, preferring his novels and sketches to the *Fairy Tales*. But their reputation grew steadily and, though Andersen maintained his deprecatory attitude, he continued to produce them, completing the first volume with instalments published in 1836 and 1837. Other series appeared irregularly till the Christmas of 1872, when the final stories were published.

Andersen died, Aug. 4, 1875, at Copenhagen.

Portrait Painter of American Birds

JOHN JAMES AUDUBON

ARTISTS have criticized Audubon's work as too photographic and scientists as too emotional and impressionistic, but the fact remains that no one of his time outshone him either as an ornithologist or portrayer of the New World's birds as they really look and act. His great work, *Birds of America*, made them famous.

Born Apr. 26, 1785, in Santo Domingo (now Haiti), Audubon studied at a military school and later an art school in France. Even then his primary interest was nature, but a year (1804) spent hunting and drawing birds on his father's farm near Philadelphia actually set the pattern of his life.

First, however, he tried a series of business enterprises, all of which were failures. From a hardware store in Louisville, Ky., and from other similar commercial efforts, he was continually attracted into the forests to observe and draw wild life. Finally, in 1819, his wife persuaded him to let her take over most of the family financial responsibilities and to devote himself altogether to what was obviously his proper calling.

He traveled down the Ohio and Mississippi Rivers, gathering material and drawing. In 1824 he tried Philadelphia, then the publishing center of America, for reproduction of his work. Failing, he went to England two years later and, with the help of Sir Walter Scott, found recognition, including election to the Royal Society of Edinborough. There Robert Havell, Jr., engraved the 435 hand-colored plates that went into *Birds of America*. It was published in parts between 1827 and 1838.

He returned to the United States to do a shorter version of *Birds of America* and to start a new work called *Viviparous Quadrupeds of North America*. Half of the drawings for the latter were completed by his two sons.

Audubon died Jan. 27, 1851. The house he built near Riverside Drive and 158th Street in New York City is preserved as a shrine in memory of the great naturalist, whose pioneering genius it was to picture birds in their natural surroundings and poses.

An unsubstantiated story intended to explain a mysterious quality about Audubon held that he was really the Lost Dauphin.

Father of Modern Science

ARISTOTLE

Perhaps no other individual has had greater influence on the intellectual life of western civilization than Aristotle. His teacher, Plato, was considered the foremost philosopher in ancient and early medieval times, but after the 12th Century Aristotle became accepted as the absolute authority in every field of thought. Even in the intellectual upheaval of the Atomic Age his influence continues as a vital force.

A Macedonian, Aristotle was born in 384 B.C., son of the court physician to King Amyntas II. As a youth he probably caught the contagious interest of his father in physiology and zoology. A background of Ionian philosophers made him meticulously thorough in his studies. And the fact that he later taught Amyntas's grandson, Alexander the Great, did not detract from his fame as a scholar.

Aristotle studied under Plato from the age of seventeen till his tutor's death twenty years later. The next dozen years he spent wandering about Greece and teaching. Then, when Alexander became king of Macedon, Aristotle went to Athens and founded the historic Peripatetic School of Philosophy, so-called because exchange of knowledge occurred while students and teachers ambled along a covered walk.

Primarily a realist, despite his training under the idealist Plato, Aristotle unearthed biological and psychological data that withstood more than two thousands years of scientific testing. His interest in government was great enough for him to write no less than 158 descriptions of state or city constitutions, all but one of which, the *Constitution of Athens*, have been lost over the centuries. Six essays on logic, named *Organon*, are considered Aristotle's most important writings. Others are *Metaphysics, History of Animals, On the Parts of Animals, Physics, On the Heavens* and *Politics*.

Aristotle died in 322 B.C. Jewish and Arabian scholars, who had absorbed his ideas in the Ninth Century A.D., returned them to the Christian world during the Middle Ages. When they began to seem an obstacle to intellectual advance, Bacon and Descartes revolted with their own philosophies, but Aristotelianism still survives.

Paragon of Novelists

HONORÉ DE
BALZAC

THE "HUMAN COMEDY" was Balzac's theme, and also the over-all title he gave to twenty years' superhumanly industrious production of novels. Marvelous powers of observation and description made many of these novels masterpieces scarcely equaled by any other writer.

Balzac's own life had drama. Born May 20, 1799, at Tours — without the distinguishing "de" which he later added to his name — he was trained to be a lawyer and even practised law for a three-year period. In 1820, however, he abandoned the legal profession and began to write in earnest. His family's objections to this course took the form of a very tiny allowance that necessitated his starving in a Paris garret.

For nine years he wrote unsuccessful tragedies, political essays and fiction. He also made disastrous ventures into business, chiefly as a publisher and printer, that loaded him down with debt for the remainder of his life. His first success came in 1829, with publication of a romantic novel modeled after Sir Walter Scott, *Les Chouans*. And the next year a powerful, though crude, melodrama called *La Peau de chagrin* won him additional attention.

A series of romantic love affairs provided Balzac with feminine prototypes for his novels. Most interesting of these was with Madame Hanska, a wealthy Polish woman, with whom he corresponded for fifteen years, seeing her only on rare occasions, and whom he finally married just five months before his death. This occurred in Paris, Aug. 18, 1850.

Despite the great success of his later novels, Balzac's income seldom exceeded 12,000 francs a year. Under continual pressure from his debts, he indulged in financial juggling that often ended in legal complications.

Not a fast writer, Balzac achieved the enormous volume of his output only by fantastic labors. He usually began work at midnight and continued for fifteen to eighteen hours at a stretch, sometimes maintaining this schedule for weeks on end. He was a meticulous craftsman and often completely rewrote a book in proof to the despair of his editors.

A few of the masterpieces comprising the "Human Comedy" are *Eugénie Grandet, La Recherche de l'absolu, Le Père Goriot, Illusions verdues,* and *Modeste Mignon.*

Founder of Modern Music

JOHANN SEBASTIAN
BACH

ACCORDING to Mendelssohn, all the worthwhile music composed since Bach could be lost and easily recreated out of the compositions written by the master during his Leipzig period alone, the last twenty-seven years of his life.

Bach became cantor of the Thomas Schule at Leipzig in 1722. For each service of both the Thomas and Nicolai churches he was required to produce a new composition. Most of them were forgotten after a hearing or two, and it is feared that many of his finest works have been lost as a result.

The little town of Eisenach, where Thirteenth Century Minnesinger Knights had their annual song contests and Martin Luther once was held prisoner, also has the honor of being Bach's birthplace, March 31, 1685. His father was town piper, and the Bach family had been important in German musical history for 200 years.

This personal background and exposure to the wonderful folk tunes of his countryside were only part of Johann Sebastian's musical advantages. When very young he was left an orphan, but his brother, Johann Christoph Bach, who owned a splendid library of the best Italian and French composers in nearby Ohrdruf, took over the younger Bach's musical education. Johann Sebastian spent so many nights copying the French and Italian manuscripts that he eventually lost his eyesight, but what he learned stood the musical world in good stead.

A violinist and organist, he first, at eighteen, played violin in the Court Band of Weimar, two years later became town organist of Arnstadt, then in 1708 returned to Weimar as music director for the Duke. In 1717 he became court conductor for the Prince of Anhalt-Cothen, whose friend, Christian Ludwig, margrave of Brandenburg, requested the six great Brandenburg Concertos, which, with the four suites for orchestra, are considered Bach's greatest instrumental work.

Bach is considered to have brought the fugue to its greatest perfection as a musical form. He did foundation work for the sonata, and raised the folk music he knew as a youth to heights undreamed of before. His choral compositions are peerless, with a dramatic content that proves he could have done operas superbly.

Married twice, Bach had twenty children, several of whom were noted musicians, the most famous being W. F. Bach, K. P. E. Bach, and J. Christian Bach. After a miraculous but brief restoration of sight he died July 28, 1750.

[19]

Founder of the American Red Cross

CLARA
BARTON

FEW MORE determinedly selfless persons than Clara Barton have ever lived. After eighteen years of teaching and five as a clerk in Washington, D. C., she gave up her job during the Civil War to distribute relief supplies to wounded soldiers. After the end of hostilities she set up a record bureau in the capital to trace down missing men and, as part of this work, identified and marked the graves of 12,000 men in the National Cemetery at Andersonville, Ga.

When the Franco-Prussian war broke out (1870), she went abroad to organize military hospitals and superintend relief on both sides of the lines. The German Emperor awarded her the Iron Cross for her efforts.

Back in the United States by 1873, she began her campaign to set up the American Red Cross and bring this country into the Geneva Convention. This was an international agreement arrived at in Switzerland in 1864 providing for more humane and standardized treatment of wounded soldiers on the field of battle. Winning her fight in the winter of 1881-1882, she became first president of the American Red Cross, remaining in that office till 1904.

At many international conferences of the Red Cross Miss Barton was the American delegate and a vigorous advocate of her own ideas. She wrote and succeeded in having adopted the American amendment to the international organization's constitution which extended its activities from wartime to peacetime emergencies as well. Then, carrying out this principle, she superintended Red Cross relief for yellow fever sufferers in Florida (1887), for flood victims at Johnstown, Pa. (1889), for the famine in Russia (1891), the Armenian massacre (1896), the Cuban War (1898), the Galveston hurricane (1900), and other disasters.

Miss Barton found time in the midst of her other duties to write several books about the society she did so much to make famous: *An Official History of the Red Cross* (1882), *The Red Cross in Peace and War* (1898), and *A Story of the Red Cross* (1904). A native of Oxford, Mass., she died in Glen Echo, Md., April 12, 1912, at the age of ninety-one.

"There's One Born Every Minute"

PHINEAS TAYLOR
BARNUM

Suckers were his business and he exploited them as no American had before him. But he began his business career with a failure.

Born in Bethel, Conn., July 5, 1810, Barnum first followed his father's example as a storekeeper, while also dabbling in the lotteries which were then an American mania. Failing in business at the age of nineteen, he next tried a weekly newspaper in Danbury, calling it *The Herald of Freedom*. It wasn't till 1835 that he found his real place in life, as a showman.

That year he bought a Negro slave woman named Joyce Heth, whom he advertised as the nurse of George Washington, announcing her age as more than 160. Starting with her as the chief attraction, Barnum set up a small company that played all over the country successfully for four years, though Joyce Heth herself died in 1836 and was then proved to be not over seventy.

Following these tours, there were a couple of lean years. Then Barnum bought Scudder's American Museum in New York City and in 1842 made a spectacular hit with his exhibition of the famous midget, Charles Stratton, whom he called "General Tom Thumb." He toured Europe with Stratton in 1844, attracting huge audiences and earning a fortune.

By 1850 Barnum was able to guarantee the celebrated Swedish singer, Jenny Lind, $1,000 a night for 150 performances, all expenses to be paid by him. Her tour of the country was one of the great successes of show business.

In the early 1860's he was elected four times to the Connecticut State Legislature and ran unsuccessfully for Congress in 1866. Then, in 1871, he organized his most ambitious and successful undertaking, the "Greatest Show on Earth"—a super-circus, menagerie and collection of freaks that traveled all over the world, first under the name of Barnum, Bailey and Hutchinson, and later simply Barnum and Bailey's. Ringling Brothers took it over in 1907.

Barnum was author of his *Autobiography* (1854 and later editions), *The Humbugs of the World* (1865), and *Struggles and Triumphs* (1869). He died April 7, 1891, leaving a fortune valued at five million dollars.

[21]

Though Deaf
He Gave New Beauty
to Music

LUDWIG VAN
BEETHOVEN

Beethoven had many obstacles to overcome —sensitiveness about his appearance, life-long money difficulties, troublesome love affairs, and total deafness from the age of twenty-eight. Yet what he accomplished places him among the world's greatest musical artists.

Though of Flemish descent, he was born at Bonn, Prussia, Dec. 16, 1770, son of a tenor singer. His father took charge of the boy's early education in music, and Beethoven made his début as a piano virtuoso at the age of eleven. Joining his father's band organization two years later, first as accompanist, later organist and still later viola-player, Beethoven soon made a name for himself as an extemporaneous performer. In 1792 he went to Vienna to study under Haydn and Albrechtsberger, and the Austrian city became his permanent home.

Critics say that his early compositions so closely paralleled Mozart's that they could hardly be told apart. But Beethoven soon felt the need for a greater freedom of expression, a greater depth and richness of design in his music. He introduced many additions and variations to old musical patterns and techniques, with the result that his works came to have an over-all tonal quality far surpassing anything that had been written before.

Unlike many of his contemporaries, Beethoven had no royal appointments or official subsidizing for his composition. What he wrote, he wrote on his own, between jobs of playing. Yet the numbered works alone—aside from the many not honored by a numeral—come to 138. They are generally divided into three periods: (1) the Mozart-like or unindividualistic first sixteen compositions, including the symphonies in C and D; (2) those numbered from sixteen to eighty, including the third, fourth, fifth and sixth symphonies, his one opera, *Fidelio*, and many pieces of chamber music; and (3) the final part of his life work, the hauntingly beautiful ninth symphony, which he could never hear, and the wonderful later sonatas for the piano and for the string quartette. The *Moonlight Sonata* is the most popular of his works.

Beethoven died of dropsy March 26, 1827.

*Last of the Great
Classical Composers*

JOHANNES
BRAHMS

As a young man of twenty Brahms played the piano accompaniment for a Hungarian violinist named Reményi on a concert tour. One night, just before Reményi started his first number, Brahms discovered that his piano was a semi-tone below proper pitch. Without a sign of discomfiture, he performed the accompaniment—playing from memory and transposing as he went from the key of A to B flat. The great violinist, Joachim, realizing what a musical feat was being accomplished, introduced himself after the concert and the two men became life-long friends. Joachim introduced Brahms to Liszt and Schumann, and the latter wrote a famous article proclaiming Brahms the great composer of the future. Despite this favorable launching of his career, it was a long time before his music was generally understood and appreciated. Even Liszt, in the beginning, mistook him for a member of the "advanced" school.

The son of a double-bass player, Brahms was born at Hamburg, May 7, 1833. He studied under his father and later, Eduard Marxsen. His first concert was at Leipzig in December of 1853, after the meeting with Joachim, and it won him a publisher for his compositions. The following year he was made choir director for the Prince of Lippe-Detmold, but gave up the post and went on to Hamburg and Zurich. In 1863 he became director of the Vienna Singakademie, but gave up this position, too, after a few months, and did not make the Austrian capital his permanent home till 1872, meanwhile going on concert tours with Joachim and Stockhausen. Real honors came to him only in the 1880's.

Brahms was disparaged for lacking "tone color." He was himself far more interested in the organic structure of his music, and to understand it one has to understand the meaning of musical form. Once critics came to appreciate his aims they acclaimed him as "the greatest musical architect since Beethoven." Among his finest works are the *German Requiem*, the *Tragic Overture* and many songs. Brahms died in Vienna, April 3, 1897.

[23]

ALEXANDER GRAHAM
BELL

IT WAS HIS FATHER's and his own interest in deafness that led to Bell's invention of the telephone. After studying at the Universities of London and Edinburgh, Scotland—the latter his birthplace, March 3, 1847 — he came to America in 1871 primarily to promote a system of "visible speech" invented by his father.

He taught first at a school for the deaf in Boston, then in 1873 became professor of vocal physiology and the mechanics of speech at Boston University. Much earlier work in electricity, telegraphy and acoustics had convinced Bell of the practicability of the telephone, but this was his first chance for thorough-going experimentation. Assisted by Thomas A. Watson, he worked for almost three years before achieving a successful apparatus. It was March 10, 1876, when the first spoken words in history were transmitted over a wire. They were sadly lacking in dramatic quality. Bell said: "Mr. Watson, come here; I want you." But it was the beginning of an era and far more interesting transmissions soon became a common occurrence.

Bell had received a patent for his invention March 7, 1876, and, despite lawsuits by Elisha Gray and other claimants, was upheld by the U. S. Supreme Court. He organized the Bell Telephone Company in 1877. By 1915 the company had expanded sufficiently and improved its equipment enough to initiate transcontinental service between San Francisco and New York.

Commercial success with his invention failed to destroy Bell's original interest in deafness. Awarded a fifty thousand franc prize by the French Government in 1880 for his conception of the telephone, he turned the money over to the Volta Laboratory for research and invention of aids to the deaf.

Besides the telephone, Bell invented the induction balance for locating metal lodged in the human body; the photophone, an instrument that transmits sound by vibrations in a beam of light; and wax phonograph records. Equally interested in aviation, he started the Aerial Experimental Association in 1907. It was under this organization's aegis that Glenn H. Curtiss made the first public, mile-long flight of an airplane in the United States (1908). Bell died Aug. 2, 1922, at his summer home in Nova Scotia.

"His Soul Goes Marching On"
JOHN
BROWN

ONE OF THE most fanatical of all the New England abolitionists before the Civil War, "Old Brown" perhaps did less to precipitate the bloody internecine conflict than his sensational attack on the Government arsenal at Harper's Ferry, Va., was given credit for at the time. But his was certainly an attitude and a lifelong course of action that helped to bring war about.

A Torrington, Conn., boy, born May 9, 1800, John Brown tried a variety of occupations—land surveyor, sheep raiser, wool trader, tanner and farmer—with meager profit in any of them.

Antipathy against slavery became one of his prime emotions when he was very young, but his early hope for emancipation lay in education, and in 1834 he made elaborate plans for a Negro school. In 1839 Brown and all his family swore a solemn oath to struggle for abolition. During the next ten years five of John Brown's sons went to Kansas, where the slavery issue was in particularly hot dispute, and he joined them in 1855. Quickly becoming chief of the anti-slavery element, "Old Brown" on May 25, 1856, instigated and led the "Pottawatomie Massacre," in which five pro-slavery men were murdered.

The Harper's Ferry incident came as the result of a long-planned scheme for freeing Virginia slaves. The idea, which had support from such prominent Northern abolitionists as Theodore Parker, was to occupy some defensible mountain position with armed men and from there to make raids on slaveholders in the surrounding country, with the hope eventually of a general uprising of the Negroes. Attacking a government arsenal was Brown's idea. He and nineteen others carried it out on Oct. 16, 1859.

Surprise brought them initial success and they held the arsenal for two days, before U. S. troops under Robert E. Lee forced their surrender. Brown was wounded in the fighting. Swiftly convicted of treason and murder, he was hanged Dec. 2 at Charleston, Va. (now W. Va.).

A popular Union Army song during the Civil War (still sung) commemorates his spirit, if not his wisdom:
"John Brown's body lies a-mouldering in the grave,
But his soul goes marching on."

[25]

Frontiersman, Pioneer and Hero

DANIEL
BOONE

ALTHOUGH many of the traditional heroic stories about Daniel Boone belong actually to other pioneers, his own life justified the supreme place he holds in our folklore as a trail blazer, hunter and Indian fighter.

Born of Quaker parents, Nov. 2, 1734, on a frontier farm near what is now Reading, Pa., Daniel Boone had only enough schooling to read and write a little and do simple sums. This lack of education was to stand him in bad stead later. After moving with his family to the Yadkin Valley, he served during the French and Indian War as a wagoner and blacksmith with General Braddock's disastrous expedition against Fort Duquesne (Pittsburgh), Pa. Along with George Washington he escaped the enemy ambush which occurred at the Monongahela River in 1755.

Ten years later, as a hunter and trapper, he reached Florida and made up his mind to settle there. But in 1769 the enterprising land speculator, Judge Richard Henderson, hired him to explore the fertile new territory of Kentucky,

to help negotiate its purchase from the Cherokee Indians, and to guide new settlers in through the Wilderness Road. Although other white men had preceded him into the "dark and bloody ground" and thus disproved the legend that he discovered Kentucky, Boone's courage, resourcefulness and perseverance were largely instrumental in settling the area. But his incautiousness about titles and taxes—a result of his lack of education—lost him the choice lands he had chosen for himself.

He moved westward again, an old man now, this time to Missouri. It was Spanish territory then. After the Louisiana Purchase he found himself once more with a worthless land title, but this time Congress, at the behest of the Kentucky legislature, made good his claim. And Daniel Boone, at eighty was able to hunt and roam the woods of his own land. He died in 1820, probably on Sept. 26.

Plant Magician

LUTHER

BURBANK

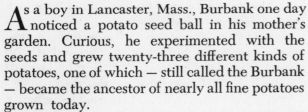

As a boy in Lancaster, Mass., Burbank one day noticed a potato seed ball in his mother's garden. Curious, he experimented with the seeds and grew twenty-three different kinds of potatoes, one of which — still called the Burbank — became the ancestor of nearly all fine potatoes grown today.

Born March 7, 1849, at Lancaster, Burbank had formal schooling only till he was nineteen, but his extra-curricular reading early included Darwin, whose *Variations of Animals and Plants under Domestication* shaped his whole career.

At twenty-one he bought a little island near Lunenberg, Mass., and set about plant-breeding in earnest. Realizing that New England soil and climatic conditions were less than ideal, however, he sold his Burbank potato to a grower and on the proceeds moved in 1875 to California. There, at Santa Rosa, he set up a greenhouse and nursery garden in which he carried on experiments for the next fifty years.

Although Burbank had no interest in proving or disproving scientific theories, his work did tend to substantiate his mentor, Darwin, on the process of natural selection. His own purpose was simply to improve useful species of plants and develop new varieties, and to this end he laboriously raised many hundreds of thousands of individual plants.

His successes were legion. Among the most celebrated are the Burbank potato, already mentioned; spineless cactus, for feeding cattle in desert areas; plumcot, a cross between a plum and an apricot; new varieties of quince, peach, apple and hybrid walnut; white blackberry, plum and new myrtle; and many flowers.

Burbank experimented longest with plums and prunes — an uninterrupted span of forty years. He spent thirty-five years on berries, evolving at least ten new varieties of commerical value. And it took him sixteen years to develop the spineless cactus.

In later life he lectured on evolution at Stanford University, and published several books, among them *Luther Burbank, His Methods and Discoveries* (1914-1915) and *How Plants Are Trained to Work for Man* (1921).

Burbank died April 11, 1926, at Santa Rosa.

Romantic Rebel

LORD
BYRON

ONE OF THE great 19th Century English poets, this handsome, wealthy nobleman lived a life as tempestuous as his imaginings.

Born Jan. 22, 1788, at London, George Gordon Byron had an exceedingly unhappy childhood. Before he succeeded to the title and estates of his great-uncle, there was little money in his family. His mother, emotionally unbalanced, alternated between spoiling him and raging at him. Infantile paralysis had lamed at least his right foot and leg. Despite the deformity, he later at Harrow became an expert swimmer and a good enough cricketer to play for his school at Lord's, later yet (May 3, 1810) successfully completing a sensational swim across the Hellespont.

Byron came into his inheritance in 1808 and promptly left Cambridge, which had done him little good, though he published his first book, *Hours of Idleness*, before his departure. In 1809 he took his place in the House of Lords, then set out on the travels through the Near East which had long been his ambition. *Childe Harold's Pilgrimage* was the result of the two-year journey and made him instantly famous. Simultaneously, he won political note, with brilliant speeches in Parliament.

A series of violent love affairs, some culminating in scandal, upset his life and ended with almost complete ostracism of Byron. He left England in 1816, never to return.

A tremendously hard and painstaking worker, Byron refused to let personal troubles interfere with his writing. He produced some of his best poetry while wandering about Europe and finally settling in Italy. *The Prisoner of Chillon* (1816), *Manfred* (1817), *Mazeppa* (1819), and *Don Juan* (the first five cantos of which he wrote between 1818 and 1821) were all done in this period. His vogue all over Europe and America as a poet was at a peak and the Continent even lauded him as a prophet of political liberty, which his own country had not done.

In the winter of 1823-1824 he decided to do something more active in the cause of liberty, and took part in the Greek revolt against Turkish overlords. Some thought he wanted a "soldier's grave." If so, he failed to achieve it, but his efforts in Greece did bring on his final illness and he died there, April 19, 1824.

[28]

Mightiest Roman of Them All

JULIUS

CAESAR

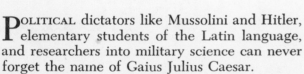

POLITICAL dictators like Mussolini and Hitler, elementary students of the Latin language, and researchers into military science can never forget the name of Gaius Julius Caesar.

A patrician by birth (July 12, 102 B.C.), he nevertheless staked his political fortunes from the start on a people's party, and all his life devoted attention to the problems of the poor, not only in Rome but the provinces. He also—particularly during the aedileship to which he was elected in 65 B.C.—spent huge sums of money on public games and public buildings, a form of advertising not lost on his imitators.

Caesar had his first taste of battle (81 B.C.) in the East, where he helped stamp out resistance to Roman rule in the province of Asia. On the death of Sulla (78 B.C.) he returned to Rome, but found the political situation unsuitable and started back East to study rhetoric at Rhodes. Pirates captured him on the way. While waiting to be ransomed, Caesar calmly promised to come back and crucify them. It is an early mark of his life-long firmness that, on being released, he promptly did so.

During the third Mithridatic war, after raising volunteers in Asia, he returned to Rome. His party had little influence, however, and it re-

quired much slow and devious maneuvering for his political advance to get underway. Finally, in his province of Further Spain he made a real start on his military reputation and restored his finances, shaky from the expenses of his aedileship. By 60 B.C. he was again in Rome and, with Pompey and Crassus, formed the first Triumvirate.

To get a military command Caesar had himself appointed governor of Cisalpine Gaul and Illyricum. The long conflict with German tribes which began soon after provided material for the only book of Caesar's remaining to us, his *Commentaries on the German War*, familiar to everyone who has studied Latin. Among his northern achievements were two invasions of Britain (54 and 55 B.C.), neither of which was a major operation or had a lasting effect.

Crassus died in 53 B.C., and Pompey went over to the Senate's political party. By 49 B.C. the Caesar-Pompey rivalry reached the stage of civil war and Caesar crossed the Rubicon with his famous statement: "The die is cast." The war was fought mainly in Spain and Africa, final victory coming to Caesar (March 17, 45 B.C.) at Munda in Spain, just a year before his dramatic assassination.

Maker of Steel—
Donator of Libraries

ANDREW

CARNEGIE

ANDREW CARNEGIE'S business career was a typical American success story, but his philanthropies were in a class of their own.

Born in Dunfermline, Scotland, Nov. 25, 1835, Andrew came with his family in 1848 to Allegheny, Pa. His first job, as a bobbin boy, paid $1.20 a week. A little later he went to a Pittsburgh telegraph office as a messenger, taught himself telegraphy and by 1853 had risen to be private secretary and telegraph operator for a Pennsylvania Railroad division superintendent. By the beginning of the Civil War he had this man's job, and was able to invest money in the Woodruff Company, holder of the Pullman sleeping car patents. His profits were the start of his great fortune.

Serving in the military transport section of the War Department during the Civil War, Carnegie reorganized government telegraph lines. After 1865 he bought into several iron companies. Selling their products to friends among railroad officials was very profitable, and he made money on European stock-selling trips

and in oil. While abroad, he became interested in the Bessemer process and after 1873 concentrated on steel.

In 1901, Carnegie retired with a fortune of $250,000,000. As early as 1889, in a *North American Review* article, he had expressed the theory that a rich man's income, beyond the needs of his family, should be given back to the people as a whole "for the improvement of mankind." Acting on this conviction, he now gave all his time to the staggering benefactions that made him world-famous.

Gifts of library buildings, his most familiar philanthropy, numbered no less than 2,505 by the end of 1918. But there were many other outlets for his munificence — the Carnegie Institute of Technology at Pittsburgh, the Carnegie Foundation for the Advancement of Teaching, the Carnegie Endowment for International Peace, to mention only a few. To carry on such gifts after his death he set up the Carnegie Corporation, with an endowment of $125,000,000.

He died Aug. 11, 1919, at Lenox, Mass.

Little Mother of All the Russias

CATHERINE
THE GREAT

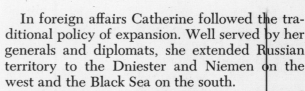

IN GERMANY she was Sophia Augusta Frederica, born at Stettin May 2, 1729, daughter of the prince of Anhalt-Zerbst. The name Catherine Alexeyevna came to her at fifteen, when she was betrothed to Grand-Duke Peter of Russia and received into the Orthodox Church.

Fifteen years of married life with moronic Peter were a miserable experience but, after the death of Empress Elizabeth, Catherine swiftly changed things. Within seven months of Peter's accession to the throne she had him removed and took over power herself. Soon afterwards Peter died or was murdered in a brawl.

Catherine's thirty-four-year reign was vigorous and economically progressive. She encouraged better agricultural methods, developed banking, reorganized the army and local administration of the government, founded hospitals and even tried—though vainly—to set up a general system of education. But, though most of her early ideas stemmed from the radical Encyclopedists who fathered the French Revolution, she accomplished less than nothing for the relief of the terribly impoverished Russian masses, and her reign was marked by innumerable peasant revolts, the chief one (1773-1775) led by Pugachev.

In foreign affairs Catherine followed the traditional policy of expansion. Well served by her generals and diplomats, she extended Russian territory to the Dniester and Niemen on the west and the Black Sea on the south.

Catherine's love affairs were numerous and colorful enough to provide material for many volumes. One of her first favorites was Stanislas Poniatowski, last king of Poland, and one of her last was the celebrated Potemkin. But she was always the dominant partner in these relationships and never let them interfere with her true purposes.

Her overpowering energy often kept Catherine at work for fifteen hours on end. Besides her political activities, she carried on a huge correspondence (her side of which was usually clever and witty), wrote many comedies, proverbs and stories, and read omnivorously.

She died of apoplexy, Nov. 10, 1796.

*The Pathfinder
of the Rockies*

KIT

CARSON

As a pioneer of the Western plains Kit Carson holds a position in American legend comparable with that of Daniel Boone in an earlier era. The same hair-raising stories — near-fatal, one-sided battles with Indians, astonishing resourcefulness against the rigors of nature, almost incredible exploits in tracking and hunting — are told about both men.

Christopher was born Christmas Eve, 1809, in Madison County, Ky., but his family moved west to Missouri in 1811 and by the time he was sixteen Kit had developed enough adventurousness to desert a prosaic saddler's apprenticeship and run off with a Santa Fé caravan.

He struggled several years for a meager living in the neighborhood of Taos, N. M., and then in 1829 went with Ewing Young's trapping expedition to California. Returning briefly in 1831 to Taos, Kit next turned northward to the beaver country, traveling with Thomas Fitzpatrick. Ten years' trapping in this area produced many of his most famous adventures.

On a Missouri steamboat in 1842 he met John C. Frémont, then only a lieutenant and engaged in his first expedition to the West. Carson went along as a guide, not only on this but Frémont's later expeditions. It was during the third one (1845-1847) that war with Mexico occurred. Carson fought under General Stephen W. Kearny, surviving the disastrous defeat at San Pasqual, where he slipped with two companions through the Mexican lines to get help.

A post-war try at farming in New Mexico failed, but in 1853 Carson herded 6,500 sheep to California and sold them for more money than he had ever had before. He was an Indian agent from then till the start of the Civil War.

Commissioned a lieutenant-colonel of volunteers, he fought in the battle of Valverde, N. M., Feb. 21, 1862, and campaigned against the Navahos and Apaches, who were helping the Confederate cause. The Navahos he succeeded in corralling into a concentration camp at Bosque Redondo. For these and other distinguished services he was made a brigadier general in 1865. The next year he became commander of Fort Garland, Colo. He died at Fort Lynn, Colo., May 23, 1868.

Titan among Tenors

ENRICO
CARUSO

ALTHOUGH Caruso was born (Feb. 23, 1873) and died (Aug. 2, 1921) at Naples, most Americans felt, and still feel, that his magnificent tenor voice was a treasured possession of this country. And with good reason, for Caruso spent the best eighteen years (1903-1921) of his singing life at the Metropolitan Opera House in New York.

As a youngster he was apprenticed to a mechanical engineer. But, beginning as a choir boy at the age of eleven, he went on to study under Guglielmo Vergine, Lamperti and Concone, and fortunately made music his own choice of a career. His operatic début occurred in 1894 at the Teatro Nuovo, Naples, in *L'Amico Francesco,* but it was not till four years later that he made a notable success, this time in *La Bohème* at Milan. He sang Marcello at Milan, though his greatest triumphs in New York came in this same opera as Rodolfo.

Caruso had a lesser previous success in his native city (1896) as Alfredo in *Traviata.* Then, after Milan, he sang in St. Petersburg, Moscow, Warsaw, Rome, Paris, London, and in Germany. In 1903 he at last made his New York début,

in *Rigoletto,* and American hearers' response was so enthusiastic and enduring that he remained at the Met for the rest of his career.

Along with a special warmth of his own and great power, Caruso's voice had the purest Italian quality. He recognized this and, while owning an exceptionally large repertory, concentrated on the Italian and French schools of composition, which best suited his talents.

In addition to *La Bohème,* in which he collaborated so spectacularly with Madame Melba as Mimi, Caruso's best known New York performances were *Aida, Rigoletto, La Traviata, La Favorita, Cavalleria Rusticana, Madame Butterfly, Carmen, Faust, Lucrezia Borgia, Manon Lescaut, Le Prophète, Il Trovatore, Don Giovanni,* and *Samson et Delilah.*

Phonograph recordings brought his voice to countless homes of non-opera-goers and their phenomenal sale did much to spread American interest in good music.

On a summer visit to his native city of Naples, Caruso died of pleurisy, Aug. 2, 1921. Italian King Victor Emanuel ordered special obsequies.

The Fabulous Cynic
CASANOVA

THIS most famous of Latin lovers and adventurers did not disprove the adage that the good die young. His ever-dangerous, dissipated and often disastrous life stretched out to a full seventy-three years (1725-1798).

At the age of sixteen he escaped his first threat of prison, on being expelled from a seminary for scandalous conduct, only by virtue of his mother's influence with a cardinal, who accepted Casanova into his household. The spiritual atmosphere failed to impress him and he soon took French leave, traveling from Venice, his birthplace, to Rome, Naples, Corfu and Constantinople. Without money, he passed variously as a preacher, journalist, abbé, and diplomatist, but in truth lived always by his wits.

Returning to Venice in 1755, he was promptly thrown into jail as a spy, but got away to Paris late in 1756 and won sympathy all over Europe with the romantic story of his escape. Appointed head of the French state lotteries that same year, he quickly made a fortune, but in 1759 was off on his travels again. The Netherlands, South Germany, Switzerland, Savoy, southern France, Florence, and Rome gave him varying receptions. Voltaire welcomed him in Switzerland and the Pope awarded him the order of the Golden Spur, but Florence expelled him.

Back in Paris in 1761, he spent the next few years there, in England, Germany and Italy, then went to Warsaw, where King Stanislaus Poniatowski greeted him as cordially as had Frederick II of Prussia and Louis XV of France. Soon, however, the customary scandal developed, a duel ensued, and Casanova fled. Turned out of Madrid in 1769, he returned once more to Italy and from 1774 to 1782 was a police spy for the state inquisitors of Venice. In 1785 his old friend, Count Waldstein, made him librarian at the chateau of Dux in Bohemia and here he stayed till his death, June 4, 1798.

Author of many clever satirical writings that often got him in trouble, Casanova is best remembered for his *Memoirs*, which give a unique, racy picture of his life and times.

He Brought the Magic of Print to England

WILLIAM
CAXTON

FIRST ENGLISH disciple of Gutenberg, who invented the movable-type printing press, William Caxton learned the art of printing during a business sojourn at Cologne (1471-1472). His home for thirty years had been Bruges, then the Continental center of Anglo-Flemish trade, and it was there he set up his first press and printed his first book, *The Recuyell of the Historyes of Troye,* in 1474 or 1475.

Born somewhere in Kent, about the year 1422, Caxton was apprenticed at the age of sixteen to a rich silk merchant named Robert Large, who afterwards was lord mayor of London. Three years later, when Large died, Caxton went to Bruges and subsequently started his own business there. By 1464 he was acting governor of the Merchant Adventurers in the Low Countries, chief British mercantile association. The following year he was head negotiator for the wool trade with Philip, Duke of Burgundy. Failing in his mission then, he nevertheless was sent back to try another time four years later when the new duke, Charles, had just married Princess Margaret, sister of Edward IV. This time he succeeded and not long afterwards became a member of Duchess Margaret's household, perhaps as a commercial adviser.

It was at Margaret's request that he completed his translation of the *Recuyell.* This, *The Game and Playe of Chesse* and *De quattuor Novissimis* were the only books printed by Caxton and his partner, Mansion, in Bruges.

Returning to England, Caxton set up a press at Westminster and brought out his first known piece of English printing, an *Indulgence,* Dec. 13, 1476. In the next fifteen years he published scores of other works, for all of which he was editor and twenty-two of which he translated. Altogether, he printed ninety-nine volumes, in black letter, including Malory's *King Arthur,* Cicero's *De Senectute* and *De Amicitia,* and various editions of Chaucer, Gower and Lydgate. His most ambitious venture was the *Golden Legend,* translated by himself and published with seventy woodcuts.

Caxton died in 1491.

[35]

Melancholy Master of the Polonaise

FRÉDÉRIC FRANÇOIS
CHOPIN

THE nationally characteristic sadness that Chopin inherited from his Polish mother is said to have limited the composer largely to mazurkas, polonaises, valses and other folk dance music, for the reason that longer compositions from so melancholy a genius could not be borne. Yet he had years of human happiness with Mme. Dudevant, better known as the novelist George Sand, and was so perfectly integrated as a musician that he enjoyed material success from the very start of his career.

A father of French origin gave Chopin his name, but he was born near Warsaw, Poland, Feb. 22, 1810, and most of his early influences were Polish. His musical and general education was excellent and when he left for his Vienna début at the age of nineteen he had already become a fully developed artist. Not for him the genius's usual years of groping, periods of change and painful development—the flowering of Chopin's artistry was early and complete.

In 1831 he left Vienna for England, but stopped in Paris on the way and made it his home for life. His exquisite piano-playing almost at once made him a lion of society. It was here that he established the long relationship with George Sand that so profoundly affected his life and became the subject of so much talk and so much writing—the latter begun by the novelist's own *A Winter at Majorca.* On this island she nursed him back to temporary health when, in 1839, tuberculosis threatened his life. Their separation in 1847, Chopin said, broke up his life. Two years later, on Oct. 17, he died in the arms of his sister, who had raced from Poland to his death-bed.

His preoccupation with Polish national dance music has been explained on the ground that his country's dances are "sadness intensified." Realizing that great heights of passion, like his own, cannot be maintained for long, Chopin usually avoided extended compositions, in which his genius was incongruous, and concentrated on études and nocturnes, besides the dances. Here his lyrical talent found perfect expression.

[36]

Brawler, Goldsmith, Troubador, Boaster, Assassin and Genius

BENVENUTO
CELLINI

L IKE OTHERS of his contemporaries, Cellini had many outlets for his creative spirit. As an artificer in gold he was peerless, but he also did sculpture that even Michelangelo admired, wrote a notable autobiography, and performed military deeds that won the Pope's gratitude.

A Florentinian by birth (Nov. 1, 1500), Cellini was supposed to follow his father's profession of musician and maker of musical instruments, but at fifteen he got himself apprenticed to the goldsmith, Antonio di Sandro, and set out on his own career. In 1519 he moved to Rome and under the patronage of Pope Clement VII industriously turned out candle sticks, medals, statuettes and other things of beauty. Here, too, he distinguished himself in the defense of the city against a Bourbon attack, by his account killing both the Constable de Bourbon and the Prince of Orange with his own hand.

Returning to Florence, he concentrated for a while on gold medals, the most famous of this period being *Hercules and the Nemean Lion* and *Atlas Supporting the Sphere*. Later he worked at the court of the Duke of Mantua, in Rome (this time having to flee the city for killing the slayer of his brother), in Paris and Fontainebleau. In 1545 he retired to his native Florence, where he died Feb. 14, 1571.

Among Cellini's numerous scrapes with the law was a period of imprisonment (apparently unjust) on a charge of embezzling the jewels of a pontifical tiara. Others resulted from his many love affairs and his hot-headed willingness to join in a brawl. These he described in his memoirs—a fascinating account of his unique career and the times in which he lived.

Ranked high among Cellini's still extant works are the famous gold salt-cellar made for Francis I at Vienna; a medallion of Clement VII; a life-size silver statue of Jupiter; and a bronze bust of Bindo Altoviti, Michelangelo's favorite. Those that have been lost included a gold prayer-book cover given Charles V by Pope Paul III; a magnificent gold "button" made for Pope Clement VII; and large silver statues of Mars and Vulcan.

Bright Light in the Dark Ages

CHARLEMAGNE

A MAN who fought fifty-three campaigns against a dozen different nations could ordinarily be expected to rest on his military laurels, but Charlemagne was no ordinary man. His prodigious activity as a soldier and politician held the western Roman empire together as a political entity, but—even more important—his interest in learning and theology kept the life-blood of civilization stirring in Europe till the Renaissance could revitalize it.

Born April 2, in either 742 or 743, Charles became king of the Franks in 768, first as co-ruler with his brother, Carloman, then, when the latter died (771), as sole sovereign. His long reign lasted for forty-six years.

Most of this time he spent in warfare, but his armies were so formidable and his military genius so well recognized that his adversaries rarely put up a real fight. The Saxons, his most pertinacious enemies, were a thorn in his side for thirty-three years, but actually gave important battle only twice.

In 773 Pope Adrian I asked Charles to help in the defense against an attack by King Desiderius of Lombardy. Responding with accustomed vigor, the Frankish king soon conquered most of Italy and in 776 made it a monarchy, of which his son Pepin was crowned king by the Pope five years later. In the interim Charlemagne warred against the Arabs of northern Spain, with less success than usual, losing his rearguard at the celebrated battle of Roncesvaux, where Roland fell and created a legend.

On Christmas Day of 800, after an on-the-spot investigation of unpopular Pope Leo III, Charles allowed himself to be crowned Roman emperor by the swiftly vindicated Vatican dignitary. In the next few years he made diplomatic peace with Constantinople. And, toward the end of his life, only the Danes to his north endangered his power.

An admittedly good husband to three of his four wives, Charlemagne had children by five other women and kept a notoriously dissolute court. Nevertheless, his devotion to Christian religion was great and from it stemmed an encouragement of scholarship and the arts that bore fruit in after-times. He died Jan. 28, 814.

"Blood, Sweat and Tears"

WINSTON L. S.

CHURCHILL

To MILLIONS Winston Churchill personifies the most admirable qualities of the British people—bulldog courage that never accepts defeat, relentless energy, picturesque speech, shrewd honesty, an abiding interest both in practical affairs and the arts.

He was born at Blenheim Palace Nov. 30, 1874, son of Lord Randolph Churchill and his American-born wife, the former Jennie Jerome of New York City. Educated at Harrow and Sandhurst, he entered the British Army in 1895, serving in Cuba with the Spanish forces that same year, and later in India and South Africa, where during the Boer War he was captured and made a daring escape.

He was first elected to Parliament in 1900 as a Conservative member, joining the Liberals in 1904. Rising swiftly, he became president of the Board of Trade (1908-1910), home secretary (1910), and in 1911 first lord of the Admiralty, with instructions to prepare the fleet for war. His preparations were an important factor in Britain's successes in World War I, but he is remembered chiefly for the disastrous attack on the Dardanelles. In later years critics said it was well conceived, and failed chiefly for lack of support by others in the Admiralty.

For ten years between the wars Churchill held no post in the Cabinet and devoted himself largely to writing and painting, though his interest in public affairs continued and he repeatedly warned against the danger of Hitler. He reëntered the Government as first lord of the Admiralty on the outbreak of World War II in 1939 and became prime minister the following spring, just before the fall of France.

In the dark first years of the war, before the entry of the United States began to turn the tide, it was Churchill's brilliantly inspired speeches as much as his great administrative ability that kept England going. His leadership was an inspiration to all the nations engaged in the conflict.

In mid-1945 the Labor party took power and Churchill returned to leadership of the opposition and to writing. In March, 1946, he made a speech at Fulton, Mo., pleading for Anglo-American unity, a speech which called worldwide attention to the growing rift between Russia and the Western Powers.

[39]

*The Siren Who Won
Anthony and Caesar*

CLEOPATRA

No other woman in history has more successfully used her personal charms to further her political ambitions than Cleopatra.

Third daughter of King Ptolemy Auletes, she was born in 69 or 68 B.C. and first came to the Egyptian throne as co-ruler with her younger brother, Ptolemy Dionysus, on her father's death in 51. Three years later, Ptolemy having conspired to deprive her of regal authority, she was in Syria gathering military forces for an attempt to regain it when Julius Caesar followed Pompey into Egypt.

The Roman dictator fell quickly and profoundly under Cleopatra's spell. He helped her vanquish the armies of her brother — Ptolemy dying in the war—and afterwards placed her again on the Egyptian throne, with another brother, whom she soon disposed of by poison.

Legend has it that Caesar's and Cleopatra's union produced a son, Caesarion, whom Octavian later put to death. Certainly, they lived together in Rome from 46 or 45 B.C. till Caesar's assassination in 44. Then, aware of the Romans' disfavor, she fled back to Egypt.

Here Mark Anthony succumbed to her fascination and she used him as she had Caesar. Their long alliance, always unpopular in Rome, led finally to war with Octavian and their historic defeat at Actium (31 B.C.). The following year Octavian landed in Egypt and worked out with Cleopatra the plot that resulted in Anthony's suicide, committed in the mistaken belief that she, too, was taking her life.

Cleopatra then set her cap for Octavian, but the man who was to be Rome's first Emperor (Augustus) proved less susceptible to her wiles than Anthony or Caesar. Learning that he firmly intended taking her to Rome as a captive, Cleopatra played her dramatic last scene, killing herself (according to legend) by the bite of an asp. This was in 30 B.C., and marked the end of the Ptolemies' dynasty, Egypt thereafter becoming a Roman province.

A host of writers, from her time to the present, have found inspiration in the colorful life of the Egyptian queen, among them Plutarch, Shakespeare, Dryden and George Bernard Shaw.

All the Ancient Wisdom of China

CONFUCIUS

Probably no one, aside from the founders of religions, has influenced the conduct and thought of so many others as Confucius. Even now, 2,500 years after his birth (551 B.C.), his teachings are repeated word for word by millions of Chinese and have merged indissoluby in the great religions of Taoism and Buddhism. Yet the timeless philosopher claimed no revelations of his own; he merely gathered the wisdom of earlier thinkers and spread it among his disciples, not even writing much of it down.

Although the great veneration Chinese since his time have shown Confucianism bestows on it the force and feeling of a religion, the wise man himself concentrated on the problems of this life, believing that his "golden rule" would bring immediate rewards to its practitioners— or at least to their close descendants. His philosophy boiled down to two precepts: be true to your inner nature (which practice he called *chung*), and apply the highest principles of that nature in your relations with others (this was *shu*). He encouraged filial piety, wisdom, courtesy, courage, righteousness, propriety and other traditional virtues—but with a verbal force and an example that won converts.

At the age of twenty-one Confucius founded a school for young men eager to learn about good government and right conduct. It was on a visit to the imperial capital for this school that he met Lao-tsze, father of Taoism.

At the age of forty-seven he received a political appointment in his native Lu that gave him a chance to prove his theories of government. The results were so remarkable that neighboring states grew fearful and set up intrigues that ended in his exile for thirteen years. Returning at sixty-eight, he spent the rest of his life (till 479 B.C.) collecting and editing historical materials, as well as poems, folklore and accounts of his people's customs.

Two centuries after Confucius's death Emperor T'sin tried to destroy all his books. But later rulers venerated him, partly because their people wanted it and partly because his conservative teachings helped keep them in power.

[41]

*From Indian Fighter
to International Showman*

WILLIAM FREDERICK
CODY
(BUFFALO BILL)

ONE of the last romantic daredevils of the American plains, William Frederick Cody won his celebrated pseudonym from a prosaic contract with the Union Pacific Railroad. To supply food for construction crews working through Kansas in 1867, he killed 4,280 buffalo.

A native of Scott County, Iowa, Buffalo Bill at the age of fourteen was a regular rider doing seventy-five miles a day carrying mail for the Pony Express from St. Joseph, Mo., to Sacramento, Calif. When completion of the Pacific Telegraph Company's line to the Coast put the Pony Express out of business, and the Civil War had started, he turned to scouting and guiding for the U. S. Army, joining it formally as a private in the 7th Kansas Cavalry in 1863. After a sixty-hour, 350-mile ride through hostile Indian territory carrying dispatches for General Sheridan, he became chief of scouts for the 5th Cavalry. His post-war chore of massacring bison completed, Cody went back to the Army as a guide and scout (1868-1872), serving in the campaigns against the Cheyennes and Sioux and twice being cited for bravery in battle.

In 1872 he had two extraordinary débuts, one as a Nebraska State legislator, the other in melodrama on the Chicago stage. The more lasting success was the latter; he maintained it for ten seasons. But meanwhile (in 1876) he returned briefly to the Army as chief scout for the Bighorn and Yellowstone Expedition, and in spectacular single combat at Hat Creek killed the Cheyenne chief, Yellow Hand.

Buffalo Bill's famous "Wild West Show" was organized at Omaha in 1883 and began the perennial touring that took it triumphantly to Europe in 1887 and won huge successes at the Columbian Exposition in 1893 and the Trans-Mississippi Exposition in 1898. As a showman he also worked with General Miles in "Ghost Dance War" (1890-1891) and "Pawnee Bill," beginning in 1908.

Ned Buntline, Prentiss Ingraham and other writers made Buffalo Bill the hero of many dime novels, and he wrote a few himself, besides his autobiography. He died at Denver, Jan. 10, 1917.

King of the Navigators

CHRISTOPHER

COLUMBUS

ALTHOUGH Leif Ericson nowadays gets credit for reaching North America 500 years before Columbus, it is still the latter who holds most imaginations as discoverer of the New World.

A Genoese, born some time between 1446 and 1451, the young Italian first went to sea at fourteen, and made many voyages in the Mediterranean, to the Azores and one even to England and the northern seas before conceiving (in 1474) his great idea of the ocean crossing. His intention was to reach India traveling westward.

Years of heart-breaking effort passed, his appeals for support going unheeded in many European courts, before Ferdinand and Isabella at last and reluctantly provided for the expedition of 1492. Columbus finally set out on Aug. 3 of that year from Huelva, in his little flagship, the *Santa Maria*, accompanied by the caravels *Niña* and *Pinta*.

After a stop at the Canary Islands they sailed fearfully westward from Sept. 6 to Oct. 12 before sighting land—San Salvador in the Bahamas. Here Columbus took possession in the names of their Catholic Majesties of Castile and Leon, starting a new era in history.

On this voyage he also discovered Cuba and Haiti. On his three later voyages he touched at various West Indian islands, discovered Trinidad and the South American mainland, and explored the Gulf of Mexico's southern shores.

From these expeditions Columbus acquired wealth and glory, though he was once returned to Spain in irons by order of Hispaniola's royal governor. Two years after the final voyage he died at Valladolid, May 20, 1506.

Many myths crowd around Columbus's memory. Besides Genoa, his true birthplace, Spain, Portugal, Germany, France, England and Greece have claimed him as a native. Then there is the legend that he had to convince scholars that the Earth is round, whereas their real objection was to his estimate of the ocean's width— and they were nearer being right than he.

But as to his navigating skill no one has a doubt. Relying only on the crude instruments of his day, Columbus once sailed the thousands of miles east from the West Indies and made a landfall only thirty-five miles from his target.

[43]

Painter at Twilight

JEAN BAPTISTE
COROT

ALTHOUGH one of the leading lights of the "Barbizon School" of painting, Corot neither suffered the economic hardship and lack of early appreciation that wounded Millet and Rousseau, nor did he arrive at their artistic philosophy by the same environmental route.

With parents who were successful milliners in Paris (his birthplace, July 16, 1796), his mother being court modiste under Napoleon Bonaparte, Corot had no youthful money troubles. There was family difficulty over his choice of profession, but when he finally wore down parental resistance, the capitulation included an annual allowance, training by Victor Bertin and Michallon, and several trips to Italy.

Up to 1843 Corot had painted in the classicist style of his teachers, with an arbitrary eye for form and arrangement. Then, coming under the romantic influence of the Barbizon artists, he suddenly realized the beauty of French landscapes from a more natural point of view and made a radical change in his methods. Critics admire his later period for "breadth of tone" and "an approach to poetic power."

But Corot had least of the realism of the "Barbizon School," the sort of realism Millet meant in his statement: "I try not to have things look as if chance had brought them together, but as if they had a necessary bond between themselves . . . the people . . . to look as if they really belonged to their station, so that imagination cannot conceive of their ever being anything else." Corot frequently did his landscapes from memory in the studio, preferring twilight to work in. Greens, grays and browns were the subdued colors of these tone-poems. He also did a number of figure paintings, some of the later examples of which are now highly valued for their strength and purity of color, combined with a classical simplicity of form.

Corot made a great deal of money painting and became celebrated for charitable gifts. During his last ten years, as "Père Corot," he was a beloved figure in Paris. He died Feb. 22, 1875.

Leather stocking Taleteller

JAMES FENIMORE
COOPER

As a wealthy Westchester country gentleman, James Fenimore Cooper had no economic need to write. Luckily for hosts of readers all over the world, he would not refuse a dare and produced his first novel, *Precaution* (1820), on a challenge by his wife. Luckily, too, for a man who needed obstacles to goad him on, it was a very bad book, imitating English novels of country life. Promptly recognizing that he should write about things he knew, he next published *The Spy* and at once scored a huge success.

Born Sept. 15, 1789, Cooper spent his boyhood on the edge of the frontier at Cooperstown, N. Y., there acquiring background for his Indian stories. After being expelled from Yale College, he became a merchant seaman, then entered the U.S. Navy as a midshipman, serving one winter on Lake Ontario. His seafaring provided material for *The Pilot*, first of the great school of blue water stories to which Melville, Stevenson and Conrad later contributed. Not until Cooper had anyone thought a tale about the sea would interest American readers.

Although he was thirty before creating his first novel, the Westchster squire crammed into his lifetime a prodigious amount of writing— more than thirty novels, many travel books and vast quantities of shorter pieces. Most famous of his works were the Leatherstocking Tales— *Last of the Mohicans, Pathfinder, Deerslayer, Prairie* and *Pioneers*. They won him a lasting reputation not only in the United States, but all over Europe, and were even translated into Turkish and Persian and Egyptian.

Cooper lived abroad for seven years (1826-1833), then returned to Cooperstown for the remainder of his life, which ended Sept. 14, 1851. His later years were embittered by widely publicized quarrels with newspapers and innumerable suits for libel.

A political liberal, Cooper was criticized for publicizing his opinions in the romantic novels. His literary style was not distinguished, and his characterizations often lacked subtlety. But he could reproduce the fascinating New World out-of-doors and he could tell a robust story. For these qualities he will long be remembered.

Lord Protector of England

OLIVER

CROMWELL

Tʜᴇ ꜰᴀᴄᴛ that Cromwell came to power fighting Parliament's battles against Charles I, then made a mockery of it as a representative body, suggests hypocrisy. But there was a great deal more in the situation than a contradiction, and for his own conscience Cromwell always had an honest answer. Appropriately for a time of acute religious strife, his answer was the will of God. The trouble, both for his contemporary enemies and later critics, was that the Puritan soldier believed firmly in his own ability to interpret the Scriptures and even more firmly that God used him as a direct instrument of the Divine will.

Cromwell was born in 1599, not long after the authoritative religious tie with Rome was broken, and long before the individual's authority over his religious conscience became a widely accepted thing. Authority was an issue in the political sphere, too; disorders between 1640 and 1660 were said to prove that the King could not govern England without Parliament, and Parliament was equally incompetent without a king. Cromwell tried to fill the impossible gap, never quite taking the throne, and never quite permitting a representative legislature.

As a military man he had solid success. Starting in the first Civil War with a troop of sixty horsemen from Cambridge in 1642, he was consistently a factor in Parliamentary victories right through the vital battle at Naseby in 1645, which was his personal triumph as a cavalryman, proving his personal theory that sternly religious-minded yeomen could beat the reckless cavalier courage of Royal horsemen. In the second Civil War (1648) he was commander-in-chief and made victory quicker — but greatly lessened his glory by permitting a rump Parliament to execute Charles I, Jan. 30, 1649. A bloody campaign in Ireland added little to his laurels, but at Worcester in 1651 he defeated Charles II and the Scots with masterly strategy.

As a tactician and leader Cromwell was superb, and he had equal ability at organization of men and materials. As a statesman he had little lasting influence. As a man, despite his Puritanical religious beliefs, which led to a habitual Biblical form of speech, he was "cheerful, jovial and merry," and got along well with people.

He died at the height of his power, Sept. 3, 1658.

The Woman who Discovered Radium

MME. MARIE
CURIE

IMPORTANT scientific discoveries are often so laborious and obscure in significance that they have no immediate dramatic import on the layman. In the case of radium, however, though its utility was not widely understood, the fantastic difficulty of refining a minute quantity from tons of pitchblende caught the popular imagination and brought early fame to Marie and Pierre Curie, who first succeeded in accomplishing the memorable feat.

This ideally suited pair were married in 1895. Marie first studied under her father in Warsaw, where she was born, Nov. 7, 1867. Because of involvement in a students' revolutionary organization she left Warsaw, went to Cracow and then to Paris, meeting her future husband at the Sorbonne. The year after their marriage she read about the experiments of Henri Becquerel with radiation from uranium salts. Her instant interest determined the lives of both Curies, for physicist Pierre joined in her work less than two years later.

Marie found that the element thorium gave off rays like those of Becquerel's uranium and named the phenomenon radio-activity. Next, in testing the power of uranium rays given off by pitchblende, she decided that there was some other element in the ore more radioactive than the uranium. Within a year the Curies detected not one but two new elements in the ore—polonium and radium. But it took them four more years of incredible labor to produce one-tenth of a gram of actual radium chloride, to determine its atomic weight, and thus prove their discovery to the world.

The Curies were immediately showered with honors, including the 1903 Nobel prize in physics, which they shared with Becquerel. After the death of her husband in 1906 Marie continued her work with radium and again won the Nobel prize in 1911. An even greater honor, perhaps, was the appointment to succeed her husband as physics professor at the Sorbonne: she was the first woman in history to hold such a position at any French university. She died July 4, 1934, at a sanitarium in the Alps.

He Traced the Origin of Man

CHARLES ROBERT
DARWIN

IT WAS THIS inspired naturalist who conceived the idea of evolution—the process of natural selection—which explains scientifically the many different species of life on our planet. He said changes occur more or less spontaneously in the form of a plant or animal; when they are favorable to environment the variation lasts; when unfavorable it disappears.

He was born at Shrewsbury, Feb. 12, 1809, grandson of Josiah Wedgwood, famous pottery maker. First sent to Edinburgh to study medicine, Darwin turned out to be unfitted for this profession and changed to Cambridge, where his father wanted him to prepare for the ministry. The friendships he formed at Cambridge, however, led him to science.

Graduated in 1831, he was appointed naturalist for a surveying voyage of the *Beagle*— a voyage that lasted nearly five years and took him around South America and to many of the western Pacific islands. Observations of living animals and fossils in the varied areas he studied on the voyage led inevitably to his theory of natural selection. But it was not until 1859 that Darwin published his celebrated *The Origin of Species*, though he had sketched the theory in an unpublished essay fifteen years earlier.

A storm of controversy greeted *The Origin of Species*, with T. H. Huxley acting as Darwin's chief defender and Bishop Wilberforce of Oxford the chief opponent. Darwin's second most famous book, *The Descent of Man*, appeared in 1871. Applying his evolutionary theory in an effort to find the ancestors of man, this work reached a more popular audience and caused even more widespread debate. Three years before he had published *The Variation of Plants and Animals Under Domestication*, which influenced Luther Burbank so profoundly. He had many other books to his credit.

Darwin died April 19, 1882, and was buried in Westminster Abbey.

The Poet of the Damned
DANTE

UNIVERSALLY accepted now as one of the half dozen greatest writers of all time, Dante, like so many of his Italian contemporaries, was a man of multiple and vigorous interests. He had some skill at drawing, took a profound delight in music and mastered all the sciences of his day. Moreover, he was on occasion a soldier and played an active part in Florentine politics.

Dante's family was moderately wealthy and well established in Florence when he was born in 1265. He was able to attend universities not only at Florence, but at Bologna and Padua, where Boccaccio says he was a conscientious student of moral and natural philosophy.

Dante associated himself in politics with the Guelf or middle class party, which was opposed by the Ghibellines, representing the nobility and upper classes. At the Battle of Campaldino (1289), in which Dante fought as a Guelf cavalryman, the middle class forces won and took over Florence's government. In 1300 he served briefly as one of six governors of the city, and it was as a result of opposition then to the Pope

that he was banished from Florence March 10, 1302. He never again entered his beloved city.

Unhappy though he was, wandering homeless through Italy, Dante produced most of his great writing after the banishment. His greatest work, the *Divine Comedy,* was completed only a short while before his death in 1321, probably at Ravenna, where his poet-philosopher friend, Guido da Polenta, was lord of the city. Of his famous poems only the *Vita Nuova* belongs to his Florentine period. This immortalized his childhood love for Beatrice.

The *Comedy* is unique in literature. For scholarship, imagination, satire, political wisdom and religious feeling, it has no equal; critics say it could have been written in no other time and by no other man. It even used an entirely new verse form, the *terza rima,* which Dante devised and which authorities say has never been surpassed, except possibly by the ancient hexameter, for varieties of expression, from straight narrative to trenchant epigram.

[49]

"*A Naked Flame of Natural Genius*"

CHARLES
DICKENS

H<small>IS NOVELS</small> were not novels in the ordinary sense, his characters violated most of the canons even of caricature, he mixed pathos and humor and social criticism in a wild witches' brew that no one else could have made into art, and he stands unique in English literature. Only Dickens is Dickensian.

A superhumanly acute eye for observation was his birthright, and there was very little else. Born Feb. 7, 1812, at Landport, he had the prototype of immortal Micawber for a father and of Mrs. Nickleby for a mother. He learned about debtors' prison from the senior Dickens's misfortunes and about child labor from his own experience in a blacking warehouse, where he tied and labeled pots when thrown on his own resources. "Something turned up" for his father once—an unexpected legacy—and Charles went very briefly to a private school, but he learned much more when the family drifted to London and he worked first as a clerk for an attorney, then later, and more happily, as a newspaper and Parliamentary reporter.

The earliest budding of his humorous genius came in *Sketches by Boz*, published first in the *Monthly Magazine* and *Evening Chronicle* and later in book form (1836). Instant popular success brought him an invitation to write the commentary for a series of humorous drawings by Robert Seymour, and this minor commercial enterprise he expanded into the marvelous *Pickwick Papers*.

An unhappy marriage failed to stem the flow of his books. *Oliver Twist* came next, then *Nicholas Nickleby, The Old Curiosity Shop, Barnaby Rudge* and *Martin Chuzzlewit*. What is generally accepted as his masterpiece, *David Copperfield*, appeared in 1849, followed by *Bleak House, Little Dorrit, The Tale of Two Cities* (his least characteristic, though structurally most artistic, work) and *Great Expectations*.

Writing always in haste to meet the deadlines of magazine serialization (he was sometimes editor of the publication to which he contributed), Dickens committed many literary crimes, but his razor-sharp sense of the comic and his knowledge of people usually saved him and often made his work superb. He died June 9, 1870, and was buried at Westminster Abbey.

Discoverer of the Mississippi

FERNANDO
DE SOTO

GOLD-MINDED, like so many of his 16th Century Spanish compatriots, De Soto came first to America in 1519, at the age of twenty-three, with his foster-father, Don Pedro d'Avila. It is said that d'Avila's harshness toward the natives disgusted De Soto enough to send him back to Spain, but his own later conduct would have made the Indians dispute this point.

He explored the shorelines of Yucatan and Guatemala in 1528, and in 1532 took 300 men to reinforce Pizarro in Peru. Here he was a considerable factor in the conquest of the Incas. He found a vital pass through the mountains to Cuzco. He helped to capture and hold Atahualpa. And for himself he garnered 180,000 ducats, with which he returned to Spain, built a mansion, married d'Avila's daughter and became a favorite at court.

Hearing exaggerated tales of Florida's riches (the name, Florida, then applied to a far larger territory than the present State), De Soto sold some property, got from Charles V a commission as "*adelantado* of the Lands of Florida," recruited a small army of 620 infantry and 123 cavalrymen, armed four ships and sailed from San Lucar in 1538. He landed at Havana and lay over there till May 12, 1539, when he embarked for Espíritu Santo Bay on the west coast of present-day Florida.

Again, the object was gold. De Soto and his men searched for it greedily and with increasing cruelty to the Indians. For four years they roamed the wilderness, journeying north into Georgia probably as far as 35°, then south to the vicinity of what is now Mobile, Ala., and finally northwestwards towards the Mississippi. They reached the great river in 1541.

Crossing, they spent the winter in territory that is now Arkansas and Louisiana. In 1542 De Soto began to retrace his steps, but at the Mississippi fell ill and died, still without finding a single nugget of the gold that had led him to a far more important discovery. His men buried him, appropriately, in the river, and went on down it to the Gulf and from there home.

The Fourth Musketeer

ALEXANDRE

DUMAS

THE AUTHOR of *The Count of Monte Cristo* and *The Three Musketeers* was an advance agent of the modern literary factory, in which a man with ideas and a name hires other men to put them down on paper and sells the product as his own — on a mass-production basis.

Like Alexandre's son, Alexandre's father was born out of wedlock, issue of the Marquis de la Pailleterie and a Santo Domingo girl named Dumas. The father became one of Napoleon's most distinguished generals, but made the mistake of disclosing his derogatory opinions about the Egyptian campaign and was retired. His son, Alexandre, was born July 24, 1802.

General Dumas died when Alexandre was four and, though his widow appealed to Napoleon, there was almost nothing with which to educate the child. When he went to Paris, at twenty, to seek his fortune, he had twenty francs in his pocket. His first job was as a clerk for the Duke of Orleans.

Beginning with short stories (a volume appeared in 1826), Dumas had his first real triumph as a writer with a romantic drama, *Henri III et sa Cour*, which was presented Feb. 11, 1829, by the Comédie Française. Orleans gave him, by way of commendation, the post of librarian at the Palais Royal. From this and the increasing profits of his prolific writing Dumas was able to establish himself extravagantly among the élite.

The demand for his work became so great that Dumas employed other writers to compose stories from his outlines, though he usually seems to have been personally responsible for their final form. His luckiest association of this kind began in 1839, with Auguste Maquet, who helped write the celebrated historical novels.

Dumas traveled a great deal, partly to gather material for books. He founded the Théatre Historique, chiefly to stage his own plays, and its failure, along with the expense of maintaining his mansion and a series of importunate theatrical ladies, put him deeply in debt, despite the enormous sums he made writing.

Dumas Fils came to his rescue toward the end and it was at his house that the novelist died, Dec. 5, 1870.

For England the Suez Canal

BENJAMIN
DISRAELI

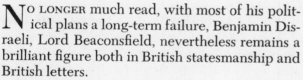

No LONGER much read, with most of his political plans a long-term failure, Benjamin Disraeli, Lord Beaconsfield, nevertheless remains a brilliant figure both in British statesmanship and British letters.

His political career could never have been fashioned except for the near-accident that his father, an Orthodox Jew, permitted him to be baptized a Christian, thus by-passing discriminatory laws of the time. Benjamin, born Dec. 21, 1804, represented only the third generation of Disraelis to live in England. Educated at a Unitarian private school and in the law at Lincoln's Inn, he took pride in his knowledge of the English character, but, as Frederick Greenwood pointed out, it was the pride of a student, not of an Englishman.

The first part of his initial novel, *Vivian Gray*, appeared in 1826, when he was only twenty-two, and became the talk of London. Two years later he ran for Parliament, but failed three times before becoming a member in 1837, first year of Victoria's long reign. Nine years and a dozen

books later he was leader of the Tory Protectionists. In 1852 he was Chancellor of the Exchequer and leader of the House of Commons. He finally became prime minister in 1868.

In domestic affairs Disraeli's ideas, such as increasing the personal power of the Crown and building a tariff around the Empire, were largely unrealistic. In foreign affairs he had the acumen to get British control of the Suez Canal, but his scheme to keep Turkey in the Balkans was not phenomenally successful and the establishment of the Habsburgs in Bosnia and Herzegovina led to World War I. Nevertheless, he performed a lasting political service to England by revitalizing the Conservative party.

Of his books *Lothair* (1870), which summed up his religious thinking, was the most successful. *Coningsby*, *Sybil* and *Endymion* contained some of his best writing. Despite a sharp wit and frequently observant realism, Disraeli was too fantastic and individualistic to gain enduring popularity as a writer. He died April 19, 1881.

Old World Composer
who Wrote
the Symphony of the New

ANTON
DVORAK

THIS wonderful musician started his career
fiddling for the village belles and beaux in
their wild dances before his father's inn at the
Czech (then Bohemian) town of Muhlhausen.
From the village schoolmaster he learned a little of more serious violin-playing, also singing.
At the age of twelve he was sent to another village to live with an uncle and had the good
luck to run into a competent musician, A. Liehmann, who was organist for the town and who
gave the youngster sound instruction in elementary music theory, piano and organ playing.
Liehmann, however, soon discovered that his
pupil had too much promise for his limited
teaching ability and sent him on to another
Czech town where he learned more under
Hancke. Then his father called him home to help
with business, and it was with great difficulty
that Dvořák got away again to Prague.

He entered the organ school of the Czech capital in October, 1857, and stayed for three years,
but parental financial support stopped after a
few months and he made his way by playing at
inns and with a private orchestra, which later
became the nucleus for the musical organization
of the Bohemian Interimstheater, where Dvořák
played for eleven years. Meanwhile, the ambitious musician had married and taken on pupils
to eke out a living, but still found time for composition, though he was so poor that a composer-
friend had to provide him with music-paper.

He said later that he had little recollection
of what he composed at this time, and many
manuscripts lay forgotten in a desk till they
were burned. He made his first bid for popular
favor in 1873, with a patriotic hymn which was
enthusiastically received and guaranteed his
later compositions eager anticipation. He wrote
an opera which failed in 1874, but the following year, on the recommendation of Brahms and
Hanslick, obtained an income from the Austrian
government that freed him from financial wor-
ries and opened his energies for a flood of new
compositions.

A series of Slavonic dances took his own country by storm. England was won in 1883 by the
Stabat Mater, later symphonies and *The Spec-
tre's Bride*. And next came New York, where
from 1892 to 1895 he headed the National Conservatory of Music. This experience happily resulted in the *New World Symphony*, one of his
most popular works. The remainder of his life
he spent in Prague, dying May 1, 1904.

"Wizard of Menlo Park"

THOMAS ALVA
EDISON

FATHER of more than a thousand inventions, foremost successful example of the "try, try again" adage, counselor to the nation on every conceivable subject, Edison was a unique and universally beloved figure in America.

Born Feb. 11, 1847, at Milan, Ohio, Edison as a child moved with his parents to Michigan and started his business career in the approved Horatio Alger manner, as a newsboy on the Grand Trunk Railway. Before long he was printing and editing his own paper in a freight car, which he also used as a laboratory for the electrical experiments that already occupied first place in his mind.

Telegraphy came next, and becoming an expert operator naturally failed to satisfy him. He invented a repeating instrument that transmitted messages on a second line without the aid of an operator; later he devised a quadruplex telegraph and a telegraphic method for communicating with moving trains.

In 1886 he set up the combination home-laboratory-manufacturing plant at Menlo Park, N. J., which was to become so famous. Here, for the next forty-five years, he toiled ceaselessly—grudging only a few catnaps' rest out of each twenty-four hours.

Among Edison's better known inventions are the phonograph, the microphone, the mimeograph, the carbon transmitter for the telephone, and his greatest gift to mankind—the incandescent bulb, which he achieved only after years of patient and discouraging effort. Edison also devised the kinetoscope, from which developed the modern motion picture. With improvements on his own invention, the phonograph, he later synchronized the two to make "talkies." The nickel-iron storage battery was his idea, and one of his last achievements was a process for manufacturing synthetic rubber from golden rod.

Almost total deafness hampered Edison's work at times, but he disparaged the infirmity, saying it saved him from distractions. He was twice married and had five children, one of whom, Charles Edison, became Governor of New Jersey. He died Oct. 17, 1931.

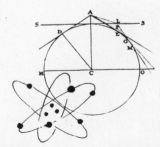

Philosopher of Physics

ALBERT
EINSTEIN

UNQUESTIONABLY one of the greatest scientific thinkers of all time, Einstein has contributed so much to understanding of the physical universe that it is almost impossible to overestimate his importance to the modern world.

Born at Ulm in southwestern Germany, March 14, 1879, he studied at the University of Zurich and taught in schools at Munich and Schaffhausen. He became a Swiss citizen and in 1901 took a job in the government patent office at Berne, continuing his studies after hours.

Prompted in part by the experiments of the American physicist, Albert Michelson, pertaining to the relative motion of matter and ether, Einstein in 1905 wrote a thesis on his special theory of relativity, which later was to be universally celebrated, if not universally understood. He argued that light must travel in all directions with equal speed, whatever the motion of the observer; that no single point can be the zero of motion, since motion depends upon the observer; that time also is relative and dependent upon the observer.

First thought of as fantastic, Einstein's theory of relativity gradually gained acceptance. He was given teaching posts at Zurich, Prague and later (1913) at the University of Berlin, where he received a comfortable income and was permitted to concentrate entirely on research. In 1919, applying his theory in the field of gravitation, he made certain astronomical calculations so much more accurate than those of Isaac Newton that he suddenly became world-famous.

Some of Einstein's other important contributions to physics are a formula for the so-called Brownian motions (relating to the movement of heat particles); a law of radiation; a light-quantum theory; and a law of photo-electric effect. He won the 1921 Nobel prize for physics.

Now an American citizen working as a mathematician at the Institute for Advanced Study at Princeton, Einstein has been active in various political causes, including Zionism. It was a letter of his to President Roosevelt that started the atomic bomb research.

Supreme Commander in the West

DWIGHT D.
EISENHOWER

Unlike some of his military associates, who helped fashion victory over Hitler and Hirohito, General "Ike" Eisenhower had the ability to win confidence and friendship, not only from bottom to top of his armies, but also from the politicians and statesmen whose ultimate responsibility those armies were. His success as a diplomat was in considerable part the measure of his success as a commander of Allied armies.

A Texan, born at Dennison, Oct. 14, 1890, Eisenhower worked his way through school at Abilene, Kansas, where his family moved from the Lone Star State, and in 1911 placed first in a competitive examination for both of the service schools; "Ike" chose West Point.

Graduated in 1915, he missed overseas duty in World War I, but made a name for himself at executive and training work. During the 1920's he was a member of the American Battle Monument Commission in Europe and later was General Douglas MacArthur's aide on the American Military Mission to the Philippines, where, as a junior officer, he was a very popular figure.

America's first large-scale peacetime maneuvers, those of 1941 in Louisiana, brought Eisenhower to the attention of President Roosevelt.

The brilliance of his planning and staff work led directly to his appointment in 1942 as head of the War Plans Division of the War Department and afterwards to command of the Allied forces in Europe. The political and military problems he had to face ranged from Darlan to Churchill, and from the relatively simple beachheads of North Africa to the bitter Battle of the Bulge—but America's first five-star general proved well able to cope with all of them. The final fall of Hitler was largely his doing.

After the war, Eisenhower retired from the Army and became president of Columbia University in New York City. During the presidential campaign of 1948, his was the most popular name in all public samplings of opinion for Mr. Truman's successor in the White House. But he steadfastly refused to be a candidate, and Mr. Truman turned out to be his own successor.

"Good Queen Bess"
ELIZABETH
THE QUEEN

A VAIN, capricious woman, who ordered the death of her cousin, Mary Queen of Scots, and her favorite, the Earl of Essex, Elizabeth was, nevertheless, one of the greatest queens of history, and certainly the most picturesque one to rule England.

The daughter of Henry VIII by Anne Boleyn, Elizabeth was born Sept. 7, 1533, at Greenwich Palace. During the reigns of her father and her brother, Edward VI, she lived quietly in the country, thirstily imbibing the "new learning" of the Renaissance. Some of it, however, was imparted to her by Protestant teachers, which roused suspicion in her half-sister, Mary, who came to the throne after Edward's death. Elizabeth outwardly accepted the Catholic faith, but when she became involved in Wyatt's Rebellion (1554) Mary had her locked up in the Tower.

On Elizabeth's accession (1558) the suspicion promptly proved justified. Supported at first by both Catholics and Protestants, the twenty-five-year-old Queen broke the ties with Rome, ordered religious services to be performed in English and established the Church of England. England became officially Protestant.

During her forty-five-year reign Elizabeth never married, but dangled the possibility of an alliance under the noses of several European potentates as a useful lure in the conduct of her devious foreign policy. Her more or less private flirtations sometimes scandalized her people and her rejection of Philip of Spain, after a long and tantalizing period of making up her mind, was a factor in his decision to attack England. But Howard, Drake, Frobisher and Hawkins routed the Armada (1588) and all turned out well.

This was one of the rare times Elizabeth resorted to force. She preferred peace and kept it for the most part by ingenious playing of her enemies against each other. Her own interest was in development of commerce and the arts. That Shakespeare and the colonization of America were of her time is significant. It was a dynamic era, marked by great discoveries in the sciences, rich literary and artistic production and a vast expansion of trade as doughty explorers opened up the New World.

The last of her line, she died March 24, 1603.

[58]

Master Scholar
of the Middle Ages
ERASMUS

At school in Daventer, Holland, his colleagues quite accurately predicted that Erasmus would be the most learned man of his time.

Born Oct. 28, 1466, probably at Rotterdam, this illegitimate son of a Dutchman named Gheraerd chose his own name and made it famous. Placed by his guardians in a monastery, he studied hard, but had no real ecclesiastical bent, and in 1492, after ordination as a priest, secured his release from the Bishop of Cambray to go to Paris.

In Paris he studied science and theology till 1497, when he went with a group of English students to the court of Henry VII. By this time his learning was distinguished and his wit and charm so pronounced that he won a highly favorable reception from the British monarch. After his return to the Continent he traveled through Italy, again being treated with great honor by dignitaries, including the Pope, who granted him a dispensation from his vows.

In 1509 he carried out a promise to go back to England, expecting magnificent favors from Henry VIII, who had come to power. Staying at the home of ill-fated Sir Thomas More, he wrote *Praise of Folly*, exposing ecclesiastical fools, and was quickly disappointed in his hopes of the king. All he got was an ill-paid professorship at Oxford. Returning to the Continent later, he died at Basle, July 12, 1536.

Martin Luther once accused Erasmus of being a coward. Unlike the great religious leader of the Reformation, Erasmus lacked militancy, readily admitting that he had "no inclination to die for the sake of truth." What he did have was prodigious erudition, a beautifully lucid literary style and a fine worldly wit.

His most notable publication was the Greek Testament, with notes and his own Latin translation. It was notable, not so much for his academic work, as for the fact that it was the first time the original was made available for comparison with the Vulgate. The *Colloquies* of Erasmus are also famous, and he left a correspondence of 3,000 letters that throw much light on his times. As editor and literary adviser for Froben's press at Basle, he made it the leader of European publishing houses.

The Sage of Concord

RALPH WALDO

EMERSON

ALTHOUGH Emerson is best remembered now for his essays, it was as a lecturer that he won influence and renown during his lifetime. On the platform he had a special charm that captivated audiences beyond the power of his graceful, simple words.

Emerson's father was seventh in an unbroken line of Puritan ministers, and Ralph Waldo, born at Boston, May 25, 1803, quite naturally gravitated to the pulpit after graduation from Harvard in 1821. Ordained in 1829, he served briefly as pastor of the Second Unitarian Church in Boston, resigning and withdrawing from the ministry over a scruple regarding church ordinances: he objected to Communion.

His first wife having died in 1832, he married again in 1835 and moved to Concord, Mass., where, except for traveling, he lived out his life. Beloved by such famous fellow townsmen as Hawthorne, Thoreau and Alcott, he became the mellow philosopher and sage who still casts a gracious spell over Concord's quiet streets.

Emerson's first book, *Nature*, appeared in 1836 and expressed the essence of all his philosophy—a belief in idealism as opposed to materialism. In 1841 came *Method of Nature* refining and developing his ideas. His first volume of essays was published in 1841 and his collected poems in 1846. Despite repeated disclaimers of subscribing whole-heartedly to its tenets, he became the accepted leader of Transcendentalism.

Before settling in Concord, Emerson went abroad to meet some of the notables he admired. Carlyle and Coleridge received him without enthusiasm. By 1847, however, his reputation had flowered so wonderfully that, on a second visit to England, the notables flocked to him.

In 1850 he published *Representative Men*, biographical essays on Plato, Swedenborg, Shakespeare, Napoleon and others, which outstripped Carlyle's similar *Heroes and Hero Worship*, at least in grace and good humor. Three years later came his *English Traits*, a penetrating but kindly critique of his British cousins.

Universally honored and loved for his efforts to give spiritual help to all men, Emerson died April 27, 1882, at Concord.

He Fathered Modern Electrical Science

MICHAEL
FARADAY

Few scientists have made discoveries of such widespread practical value as those of Michael Faraday. Without the data on electro-magnetism which he provided, our modern electrified world could not exist. Yet his brilliant research work was done practically without formal education.

Born at Newington, in Surrey, England, Sept. 22, 1791, Faraday was the son of a blacksmith who could not afford much schooling for the youngster. When very young he was apprenticed to a bookbinder. But somewhere he acquired a profound interest in science and spent all his spare time studying whatever scientific books he could obtain.

The first important step of his career came when he attended a series of four lectures given by the famous chemist, Sir Humphrey Davy. Hoping to win a chance for a job better suited to his interests, Faraday sent his notes on the lectures to Sir Humphrey, and the latter was so impressed by them that he hired Faraday as his own assistant. Faraday's early experiments, such as condensing gases under pressure, brought him

enough reputation to secure his appointment as director of the Royal Institution's laboratory in 1825. Later he took Sir Humphrey's place as professor of chemistry in the Royal Institution.

A few of his important chemical discoveries were alloys of steel, a compound that was developed into the basis of aniline dyes, and chemical methods that led to manufacture of optical glass having a higher power of refraction.

His most significant work, however, was with electro-magnetism. In more than twenty different series of researches, Faraday proved the possibility of inducing an electric current in one circuit by passing a current through another circuit; he laid the foundation for modern electric dynamos and motors by making a magnet revolve continuously around an electric current; and he labored fruitfully with electrolysis, even originating the terms "anode" and "cathode." It was on the basis of his pioneering that other physicists were able to advance the science of electricity to its present level. Faraday died Aug. 25, 1867, at Hampton Court.

HENRY
FORD

Back in 1919 Ford and his son Edsel had bought out minority stockholders for $70,000,000 and the Ford Motor Company became the strictly family affair that differentiated it so sharply from other billion-dollar concerns. Bank loans and bond issues were tabu with the elder Ford. He also disliked being dependent on others for his materials and made a policy of owning the source of everything needed for the manufacture of his car.

In 1914 Henry Ford made labor history with a minimum wage of five dollars for an eight-hour day, double the contemporary standard for a nine-hour day. He established the Henry Ford Hospital in Detroit, open to anyone, with fixed payments and salaried doctors and nurses. But he opposed charity and paternalism on principle.

In 1915, during World War I, he paid for and went along on the celebrated "Peace Ship" mission, which was intended to stop the war in Europe by a gesture, but ended in a notorious fiasco. Nominated for the U. S. Senate in 1918, he refused to campaign and lost the election.

Ford had a deep interest in American folk customs and American antiques. His opinions on many other matters were published in popular magazines, usually with Samuel Crowther as collaborator. He died April 7, 1947.

A MECHANICAL and industrial genius of well justified renown, Henry Ford took automobile manufacturing out of the backyard and made it the nation's greatest industry, his own company alone in 1926 (with its subsidiaries of coal, ore, timber, railroads, ships, etc.) being rated third for the country.

A young man at the turn of the century (he was born July 30, 1863, on a farm near Dearborn, Mich.), Ford saw the possibilities of mass production and low prices long before his competitors. Starting with a reputation for speed cars (he built the famous "999"), he organized the Ford Motor Company in 1903 and began working toward a light, strong machine with standardized parts that almost anyone could afford to buy. After a number of experiments he arrived at the Model T—the "tin lizzie" of which 15,000,000 copies were sold before Ford submitted, in 1928, to the public demand for a more luxurious product.

The Man Who
Harnessed Lightning

BENJAMIN
FRANKLIN

To this day Benjamin Franklin remains Philadelphia's first citizen, but the scope of his influence extended far beyond the Pennsylvania city. How far was indicated when he died, April 17, 1790. Not only did Philadelphia turn out en masse for the funeral and the new United States Congress pass resolutions of sorrow, but even in distant Paris the French National Assembly went into mourning for three days.

Boston-born (Jan. 17, 1706), young Franklin learned printing from his half-brother, James, who later founded the *New England Courant*. At the age of seventeen he went to work in Philadelphia. Later he bought the *Philadelphia Gazette* and as editor made a great success of it; *Poor Richard's Almanack*, first issued in 1732, was an even more profitable publishing venture. In 1731 he organized the Library Club, which grew into the first circulating library in America. Five years later he set up Philadelphia's first fire company. Street paving, a hospital, street lamps, the Academy of Philadelphia and the University of Pennsylvania were among his other civic accomplishments.

The famous kite experiments led to invention of the lightning rod, and he made a comparable contribution to mankind's comfort with the Franklin stove. Every branch of science held his interest and his innovations ranged from medical instruments to meteorology. Moreover, he was a tireless spreader of scientific knowledge not only via the printed word but also through a vast correspondence he maintained.

Franklin's national career began in 1753 with his appointment as Postmaster-General of the Colonies. Later he went to England to fight the Stamp Act. When the Revolution came he helped frame the Declaration of Independence and was one of the signers. Then he went to France to enlist aid for the American cause, succeeding far beyond expectations and becoming himself a great favorite with the French. Afterwards, he was four times President of the Commonwealth of Pennsylvania.

Franklin's brilliant writing shows best in his partly completed *Autobiography*, famous all over the world for its wit and wisdom.

[63]

A Yankee Who Sang of the South

STEPHEN COLLINS
FOSTER

IN Stephen Foster's day Negro minstrel jingles were known as "Ethiopians." In 1852, at the age of 26, Foster announced that he intended "without fear or shame to establish my name as the best 'Ethiopian' songwriter." He made the statement to E. P. Christy, who collaborated with him on *The Old Folks at Home* and with his minstrel troupe helped to popularize Foster's tunes in both the United States and Europe. No one can deny that he carried out his promise.

Born at Pittsburgh, Penna., July 4, 1826, of prosperous Scotch-Irish parents, Foster spent all but a few years of his life in that city and had no personal knowledge of the South, about which so many of his songs were written. He showed musical inclination at the age of six and his first extant composition dates back to 1840. Called *Tioga Waltz*, it was, of all unlikely things, an ensemble for flutes!

As star performer of a youngsters' Thespian Society Foster got practice with Negro minstrel jingles. Otherwise, he had little or no formal training in music. For the "Ethiopian" and sentimental "ballad," which were his twin fields of effort, not much beyond a keen ear, imagination and industry was needed.

By 1850, when he published the once enormously popular *De Camptown Races*, Foster was earning enough from his songs to give up his bookkeeping job and concentrate on musical composition. Within the next four years his fame had risen to its peak and the total of his songs had halfway reached his ultimate mark of 175. Although royalties on them were substantial, after 1860 he usually sold the lyrics and music to publishers outright, thus encouraging himself to production line methods. Most of these pot-boilers are properly forgotten today. But *Swanee River, Massa's in the Cold, Cold Ground, Old Black Joe, My Old Kentucky Home, O Susanna, Old Dog Tray* and others remain perennial and well-loved favorites.

Foster moved in 1860, to New York City, where he lived extravagantly, dissipating the large sums of money realized from his songs. He died Jan. 13, 1864, in the charity ward of Bellevue Hospital, as the result of an accident.

The Painter Who Invented the Steamboat

ROBERT
FULTON

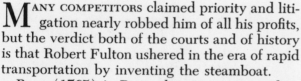

MANY COMPETITORS claimed priority and litigation nearly robbed him of all his profits, but the verdict both of the courts and of history is that Robert Fulton ushered in the era of rapid transportation by inventing the steamboat.

Born (1765) in Pennsylvania at a town then called Little Britain but later renamed Fulton in his honor, the inventor had no more than the rudiments of reading and writing for an education and was apprenticed when very young to a jeweler in Philadelphia. Here he met and became a friend of Benjamin Franklin, taught himself to paint and, in his spare time, studied and began to experiment with paddlewheels.

Finding a ready market for his landscapes and miniatures, Fulton was able to buy a farm for his widowed mother and finance a trip to London for himself. He stayed several years in England, painting and experimenting with improvements on canal navigation, then moved to Paris (1794), where for some years he worked fruitlessly on submarines. The torpedoes he tried out in connection with the submarine experiments had partial success, however, and the

British government hired him to do further work with them. Fulton finally was able to blow up a 200-ton ship with one of his models.

Returning to America, he concentrated on devising a steamboat. First interested in the idea as early as 1793, he had tried out several models in France, with indifferent luck. But the *Clermont*, built in New York in the spring of 1807, sailed grandly up the Hudson on Aug. 11 all the way to Albany, completing the trip in 32 hours and astonishing everyone who saw it.

Fulton's reputation was made at once and steamships soon began replacing sail. Before his death (Feb. 24, 1815 in New York City) he built a forty-four-gun steam warship for the United States government and was once again tinkering with a submarine, the *Nautilus*, when his end came. His invention had so captured American imaginations that the whole nation joined in a demonstration of mourning. Later a monument was designed in his memory and placed, appropriately, in upper Manhattan, overlooking the Hudson River.

[65]

Master Soldier
Minor Poet

FREDERICK
THE GREAT

During the eleven years of peace that followed he showed a wonderful energy putting his territories in order, an energy that somehow was contagious for his people. Thriftily he established Prussia's finances on a solid footing, encouraged both industry and agriculture, put honest, industrious men in public office so that the standard of justice and administration improved mightily, did a good deal to promote elementary education and to lighten the burdens of the lower classes—though in accordance with his paternalistic nature he never thought of abolishing the medieval system of serfdom. He also increased the size of his army, armed and supplied it well, perfected its organization and discipline, and was ready for his biggest military venture, the Seven Years' War (1756-1763).

Again caused by a dispute over Silesia, the war this time involved most of Europe and even had repercussions in America (the French and Indian War). Although it ended in something like a stalemate, Frederick preserved his earlier conquests and established Prussia as one of the great powers of the Continent. By the time of his death, Aug. 17, 1786, he had increased the size of Prussia by fifty per cent and, despite his wars, made it a prosperous, dynamic kingdom.

UNLIKE his brutal father, Frederick II of Prussia had a profound love of the arts and, whenever he could, surrounded himself with learned and talented men. He wrote in French great quantities of verse, none of it better than mediocre, and was musical enough to play the flute. But his notable accomplishments were in the military and political spheres.

Born sometime in January, 1712, he succeeded to the throne in 1740 after a miserable youth under the crazily rigid discipline of his father. Within a year he had begun his brilliant military career with a victory over the Austrians at Mollwitz. A second campaign against Maria Theresa, the Austrian queen, ended in 1745 with Frederick in control of Silesia, which he had coveted, and also the owner of a high reputation as a soldier.

Nature Was His Teacher

THOMAS
GAINSBOROUGH

THE MAN who painted *The Blue Boy* was one of England's greatest portrait and landscape artists and an unconscious forerunner of the school of Impressionism.

He lived a pleasant 18th Century life. Born in 1727 at Sudbury, he moved to London at fourteen to study etching under Hugh Gravelot, having already shown a talent for drawing. He also studied painting under Francis Hayman. At nineteen he married charming Margaret Burr, who made his life continually happy, and settled in Ipswich to paint portraits and landscapes. He also joined a musical club and learned to play several instruments.

Among his friends and patrons was Philip Thicknesse, who got him commissions and later wrote his biography. It was Thicknesse who persuaded him to go to Bath, then a wealthy resort town, where he painted many dignitaries. The landscapes of this period are considered his finest, and his observations of the Bath countryside inspired the remark that "Nature was his teacher and the woods his Academy."

Gainsborough moved to London in 1774, prosperous and famous enough by then to be summoned to the palace to paint King George III. He did eight portraits of the monarch, besides pictures of other members of the royal family and of such personages as Sheridan, Burke, Johnson, Mrs. Siddons, Canning, Pitt, Clive and Blackstone. The royal family likenesses are accepted as his best portrait work.

In 1768 he had been elected one of the original thirty-six members of the Royal Academy, thereafter exhibiting his pictures at the annual Academy shows till 1783, when he withdrew them, dissatisfied with the position accorded him, and later arranged his own exhibitions.

Gainsborough painted more than 500 pictures, 200 of them portraits. One of these, *Lizbeth, Duchess of Devonshire*, was stolen in 1876, carried to New York and Chicago, but recovered twenty-five years later because the thieves could not dispose of so valuable a painting. His landscapes are held to be even finer than his portraits. He died Aug. 2, 1788.

He Mapped the Heavens

GALILEO

REMEMBERED best for his telescopic examination of the stars, for his experiments with falling bodies from the Leaning Tower of Pisa and for recanting his briefs under religious persecution, this 16th Century scientific genius had many other claims to fame.

His father, an impoverished Florentinian of good family, himself an able mathematician and musician, wanted Galileo to be a doctor. The younger Galilei, born Feb. 15, 1564, at Pisa, obediently studied philosophy and medicine, though he found them not to his taste, till one day in 1581 he noticed a lamp swinging in a cathedral. Checking its steady motion against his pulse, he conceived the pendulum and promptly built a clock employing one. After this his father let him study mathematics.

Invention of the hydrostatic balance for determining the specific gravity of solids made him known all over Italy and won him a professorship at the University of Pisa. It was here (1589-1591) that he conducted his remarkable experiments with falling bodies, proving dramatically at the Leaning Tower that they drop with the same velocity regardless of weight.

In 1592 he made the first thermometer and in 1609, hearing rumors of the invention of the telescope, promptly built one of his own. The first trial brought only triple magnifying power, but he soon attained a power of thirty-two and manufactured hundreds of these instruments with his own hands for other scientists. He also used his own telescope for extraordinarily accurate observations of the stars.

Convinced from youth that Copernicus was right about the solar system, Galileo was nevertheless discreet enough to avoid ecclesiastical difficulties till publication in 1613 of his *Letters on the Solar Spots*. Discrepancies with Scriptural passages brought a papal admonition not to teach such doctrines and Galileo promised to obey. He did so obey till 1632, when, overconfident, he published more of his astronomical work. The book brought tumultuous applause from the whole civilized world, but also a command for Galileo to appear before the Inquisition. Threatened with torture, he recanted and was allowed to spend the rest of his life at his researches. He died Jan. 8, 1642.

The Mahatma
—Great Soul
GANDHI

IN A DISORDERED world that relied on force to settle issues. Gandhi was unique as a leader. Both his chief weapons were profoundly peaceful—the non-violent disobedience with which he taught his followers to oppose the British and his own dramatic "fasts until death."

A thoroughly Indian figure, Gandhi (born at Porbandar, India, in 1869) was educated in England and first practised law at Bombay and in South Africa with considerable financial success. In South Africa, however, he went actively into politics, fighting for the rights of fellow-Indians who had settled there. When a British commission in 1914 abolished the worst injustices, he returned to India for a larger battle.

He had already worked out the non-violent resistance technique. Now he turned to an ascetic religious life, wearing Indian clothes, subsisting mainly on goat's milk and symbolizing his belief in home industries for India by continually operating a hand spinning wheel. His followers rapidly increased, both in numbers and enthusiasm. By 1921 his influence was so great that the National Congress delegated all its authority to him, even the power to appoint his successor. But the campaign of "non-violent non-coöperation" he had proclaimed the year before got out of hand and produced outrages that culminated (1922) in Gandhi's trial and imprisonment for conspiracy to overthrow the government.

Released after serving less than two years of a six years' sentence, he became president of the Indian National Congress in 1925 and continued his agitation against foreign domination of his country. On several later occasions the British put him in jail, but his "death fasts" and the world-wide sympathy they evoked usually won his release and made gains for his cause. His antipathy against the British was so great that he even urged Indian support of the Japanese during World War II.

In May, 1946, the British presented a plan for Indian independence. But an assassin's bullet cut Gandhi down Jan. 30, 1948, before he could see the realization of his life's dream.

Genius of Jazz

GEORGE

GERSHWIN

For the generation following World War I no other American composer had the wide popular appeal or the suitability to his times of George Gershwin. Enormously successful on their first appearance, many of his songs have a durable quality that keeps them in high favor despite incessant repetition by dance bands, radio orchestras and the movies.

Gershwin was born in Brooklyn, N. Y., Sept. 26, 1898. Starting as a song plugger for "Tin Pan Alley," he made his way in the popular music business so precociously that his first musical comedy (*La, La Lucille*) appeared on Broadway in 1919, when he was twenty-one. And during the next dozen years he wrote some of the greatest successes in this field ever presented on the American stage. Among them were four successive editions of *George White's Scandals* (1920-1924), *Lady Be Good* (1924), *Funny Face* (1927), *Girl Crazy* (1930), and *Of Thee I Sing* (1931), which won the Pulitzer Prize.

In 1923 he made his first essay into more serious music, with *Rhapsody in Blue*. Based on the mood of familiar jazz music, it was introduced the following year at Aeolian Hall in New York by Paul Whiteman as the high point in a concert called "Ten Years of Jazz." This was one of the early efforts to raise American jazz music to a dignity comparable with that of established European forms.

In 1928 Gershwin explored a similar vein with *An American in Paris*, which was presented at Carnegie Hall in New York by the Philadelphia Symphony Orchestra, Walter Damrosch conducting, also with great success. His *Second Rhapsody*, introduced by Koussevitsky and the Boston Symphony Orchestra in 1932, had less of a vogue, despite its impressive presentation.

Perhaps his most interesting and appealing experiment was *Porgy and Bess*, an extraordinary combination of musical comedy and opera, based on DuBose Heyward's novel and play about Southern Negroes. It was an outstanding hit in Boston and New York in 1935 and has been revived a number of times.

Gershwin also wrote many individual songs and the music for Hollywood productions. He died in Hollywood, July 11, 1937.

[70]

Giant of German Literature

JOHANN WOLFGANG
VON GOETHE

Goethe was not only the greatest figure in German literature, he was also one of the most highly and variously gifted men of the 18th Century.

Son of an imperial chancellor, he was born at Frankfort-on-the-Main, Aug. 14, 1749, and sent at the age of sixteen to the University of Leipzig to study law. With his broadly ranging mind it was impossible to concentrate on legal matters and he gave most of his time to literature and philosophy. Nevertheless, after a period of illness, he completed his law studies at Strassburg, simultaneously grounding himself in chemistry, anatomy and architecture, and delving ever more deeply into classical literature.

At Strassburg he fell in love with Frederica Brion, nineteen-year-old daughter of a minister. Like other youthful affairs of the poet, it affected him profoundly, but not to the point of marriage. It was not till 1806, as a matter of fact, and then only after she had made a home for him for seventeen or eighteen years, that Goethe married Christiane Vulpius.

After Strassburg he lived briefly at Wetzlar, continuing his studies and absorbing Gothic atmosphere. Wetzlar was the scene of *Sorrows of Werther,* which brought him fame in 1774. At about this time, too, he began his many years of work on *Faust,* his poem of greatest interest to English-speaking people.

In 1775 he settled in Weimar, presiding as a kind of small statesman-literary oracle over the group gathered by Goethe's friend, the Grand Duke of Saxe-Weimar. Later he traveled to Switzerland and Italy, writing as a result *Iphigenia, Egmont, Tasso* and *Venetian and Roman Elegies.* In 1792 he took part in the unsuccessful German campaign against France, writing his recollections of it afterwards. After the death of Saxe-Weimar in 1828 he withdrew from politics and society, devoting himself entirely to writing. He died March 22, 1832.

It has been said that what Shakespeare knew, he knew; what Goethe knew, he learned. Lacking the inspired wisdom and innate poetry of the matchless Elizabethan, Goethe nevertheless had marvelous imagination, a vast learning and an almost incredibly well-rounded intellect.

From Plowboy to President

ULYSSES S.
GRANT

GRANT is the proverbial example of the man who fails at many things, but suddenly in middle life sees his main chance and leaps to immortal glory.

He was born April 27, 1822, on a farm near Point Pleasant, Ohio. At West Point, from which he was graduated in 1843, he made little mark except as a horseman. Through the Mexican War he served with moderate distinction, ending as a captain, but resigned his commission in 1854, after criticism of his excessive drinking.

Farming, real estate and a leather shop at Galena, Ill., did little more than keep his family alive, and Grant was considered a broken man when the Civil War began. Nevertheless, he got a colonel's commission with the 21st Illinois Regiment and promptly started winning battles. His capture of Forts Henry and Donelson brought him the rank of major-general early in 1862, and on April 6-7 of that year he commanded the Army of the Tennessee at the bloody but victorious battle of Shiloh. A year later he besieged Vicksburg, opening the Mississippi River to the Union.

President Lincoln made Grant commander of all the Union forces in March, 1864. Now a lieutenant-general, Grant began the final assault on Lee's armies in Virginia. Through the incredibly bloody battles of the Wilderness and Spottsylvania Court House he doggedly drove his men, relieving tension in the North with his famous words: "I purpose to fight it out on this line if it takes all summer." At Appomattox General Lee finally surrendered April 9, 1865.

After the war Grant was elected President in 1868 and re-elected in 1872, though a good deal of scandal attached to his administration. Following his second term, he made a triumphal tour of the world, then settled in New York City, where association with an unscrupulous financial house ruined him. To recoup his family's fortunes he wrote his memoirs, a charming and popular autobiography, though suffering agony all through the work from cancer of the throat. He died four days after its completion, July 23, 1885, and was buried in the familiar granite mausoleum on Riverside Drive.

Chopin of the North

EDVARD
GRIEG

THE MUSICAL movement which Grieg pioneered in Norway is not regarded as having much promise of development—for the reason that he brought it to such perfection himself.

His father, Alexander Grieg, was English consul at Bergen where the composer was born June 15, 1843, but his mother had pure Norwegian blood and from her came his talent. She began giving him piano lessons when he was six, and he wrote his first composition, *Variations on a German Melody*, at the age of nine.

At fifteen he entered the Leipzig Conservatory, coming under the romantic influence of Mendelssohn and Schumann. Then, in 1863, he moved to Copenhagen, there studying under Gade and Emil Hartmann, who were of the sentimental Scandinavian school. It was not till he met Richard Nordraak that he saw the possibilities of a tougher approach to northern folk tunes. The two agreed on a crusade for Norwegian national music and Grieg started a Copenhagen concert society to encourage young Norwegian composers.

In the late 1860's Grieg spent winters in Rome, meeting Liszt, who was enthusiastic about his piano concerto, playing it at sight from the manuscript. Christiania became his home in 1866 and in 1872 he was made a member of the Royal Musical Academy of Sweden, the Norwegian Storthing two years later awarding him an annuity of 1,600 kronen. He played and conducted in London several times during the 1880's and 1890's.

His best known work includes the famous music for Ibsen's *Peer Gynt*, the song, *Ich liebe dich*, his piano concerto and the suite for stringed orchestra, *Aus Holbergs Zeit*. Strongly nationalistic, Grieg's compositions showed fine lyrical feeling and a surely sensitive command of romantic and picturesque material. His better songs, such as *Ein Schwann* and *Solvejg's Lied* usually were in the spirit of the *Volkslied*. Not as broad in appeal or inspiration as Chopin, the northern composer nevertheless well merits comparison with this master.

He died at Bergen, Sept. 4, 1907.

[73]

The Painter
Who Loved Color
More Than Life

VINCENT
VAN GOGH

IN THE disrupted, difficult and tragically brief life of this artist there was only one person to help him with anything but advice. That was a brother, who, almost alone, believed in his genius, and, wholly alone, gave him practical aid when it was needed.

Van Gogh was the son of a Calvinist minister, born March 3, 1853, at Groot-Zundert in Brabant, Holland. An uncle who was a dealer in pictures at The Hague employed him when he was sixteen, and a more important art dealer gave him work later in London and Paris. By 1876 he was a teacher of art in England, but returned to Holland under the spur of religious inspiration. Imbued with the early Christian ideal of communism, he lived among miners. But drawing occupied his spare time and in 1880 he went to Brussels to study painting. From there he went to his father's village of Neunen and spent some years painting the simple life of the peasants. His celebrated *The Potato Eaters* (1885) is a product of this time.

After a little study in Antwerp, he joined his brother, Théo, in Paris, and was persuaded by members of the Impressionist and Neo-Impressionist schools to forego his previous browns and umbers and strike out with the clear, bright colors of Seurat. A result was *The Restaurant on Monmartre*, his first venture into the luminous style for which he is now famous.

Two years of Paris were enough for Van Gogh and in 1888 his brother paid his way south, to Arles in Provence. Here he painted himself, the postman, the innkeeper's wife, the fruit trees, the sunflowers, the fields bathed in sunlight. Color became an obsession with him.

The painter, Gauguin, arrived for a visit and the two worked awhile together. Then one day Van Gogh threatened his friend with a knife, for no reason other than the torments of his own disturbed mind, and in repentance cut off his own ear. The rest of his life, though he continued to paint beautifully, was spent under watchful care or in institutions. Nevertheless, he shot himself and died July 20, 1890.

His Printing Press
Brought Learning
to the Masses

JOHANN
GUTENBERG

FEW MEN of relatively modern times and great importance have left a more meager record of their lives than Johann Gutenberg. His creation of the movable-type printing press, by making it possible to spread knowledge quickly and easily, as much as any other invention, made possible the modern world. But the wonderful recording method he devised for other matters was never used to keep a history of his own activities, and no one today knows when or how he arrived at his epoch-making discovery.

At the German city of Mainz, perhaps in the year 1398, the inventor was born of aristocratic parents who used the names Gutenberg and Gensfleish from two of their estates. Probably expelled from Mainz, the family moved to Strassburg and there, in 1434, Johann had the first of several encounters with authority over a debt. This time it was one owed to him. He apparently seized and held the town clerk because of money owed him by the city, and freed him only at the plea of the mayor and councilors.

A partnership set up in 1438 with Andreas Dritzehn and Andreas and Anton Heilman,

which shortly led to litigation, gave the first clue to Gutenburg's invention, since the word "printing" appeared in the court records. Between 1444 and 1448 he disappeared altogether. But in 1450 another partnership was recorded, this time with Johann Fust.

Fust undertook to advance Gutenburg 800 guilders, on the security of printing tools Gutenburg was to make, and to give him 300 guilders a year for expenses. Both partners failed to keep their promises and as a result of a lawsuit in 1455 Fust removed the plant to Mainz, where he worked with Schöffer till Adolphus II sacked the city in 1462. During their five years of partnership Gutenberg apparently printed several small books, a papal letter of indulgence, part of a large folio Latin Bible and a dictionary or vocabulary called *Catholicon*, which has been lost. The Mazarin Bible attributed to him was more likely printed by Schöffer, Fust's partner.

Except for evidence (another lawsuit) that he was still engaged in printing at Mainz in 1468 and that he died sometime that year, little else is known about Gutenberg.

"...but One Life to Give for My Country"
NATHAN
HALE

Many spies of many nations have been shot, buried and forgotten. Nathan Hale is remembered both for his gallant last words, "I only regret that I have but one life to give for my country," and also because the life he gave was so young and so promising.

A Coventry, Conn., boy, he was born June 6, 1755, raised on his father's farm, and educated at the local school and Yale College, entering the latter at the same time as his older brother, Enoch. Often referred to as the "flower of the family," he achieved wide popularity at Yale. He was made secretary of the Linonia debating society and spoke frequently and acceptably at its meetings. An excellent student, he was graduated with honors in 1773.

His talent for teaching, after less than a year at East Haddam, Conn., gained him a post in the Union School at New London that paid the then considerable sum of $200 a year. He made many friends in New London and enjoyed his work, but promptly left both in July, 1775, to become a first lieutenant in the newly created Seventh Regiment, which joined Washington in his siege of the British at Winter Hill, near Boston. When the Red Coats evacuated Boston by sea for New York, Hale was with the first American units that attempted to reach the city overland before them.

General Howe landed on Long Island in July of 1776 and fought Washington late in August, but Hale's regiment did not participate. When the American commander asked for a volunteer to go through the British lines for information on the enemy's strength and plans, Hale, now a captain, stepped forward.

He crossed the Sound from Norwalk to Huntington and penetrated the enemy lines disguised as a Dutch schoolmaster. That much is known, but whether or not, during the following week, he succeeded in relaying back any useful information is unknown. On Sept. 22 the British announced in New York that he had been executed as a spy that morning.

The courageous dignity with which he met his death endeared Hale to all Americans, and made his name one to be remembered in the history of the nation's heroes.

He Crossed the Alps to Battle Rome

HANNIBAL

THE SECOND PUNIC WAR (219-201 B.C.) ended in victory for Rome, but it won eternal military glory for the Carthaginian commander, Hannibal. Against numerically superior Roman land forces, with his supply routes at the mercy of a powerful Roman navy, he yet maintained a hold on northern Italy for sixteen years.

Hannibal went on his first expedition (238 B.C.) with his father, at the age of nine, and before starting took an oath of hatred toward the Romans that dominated his whole life. He came to command of the Carthaginian army at twenty-nine, and immediately began the great conflict with an attack on Saguntum.

Leaving his younger brother, Hasdrubal, to hold Spain, Hannibal outmaneuvered the Romans at the Rhone River and crossed the Alps into northern Italy without opposition, though his losses on the terrible mountain march were very high. One brilliant victory after another soon gave him control of northern Italy.

In 217 B.C. he crossed the Apennines and surprised the Roman commander at Lake Thrasimene, overwhelming his army, and went on to sweep the Adriatic coast as far as Apulia. The next year he captured a huge supply depot at Cannae and routed an army of 50,000 under Lucius Aemilius Paulus and Gaius Terentius Varro. A later effort to take Naples failed, but he did take Capua, second biggest Italian city.

Now Fabius the Delayer took charge of Roman strategy and began avoiding pitched battles with Hannibal (who always won them anyway), unless he had overwhelming numerical superiority. The process of attrition wore down Hannibal's strength, and when Hasdrubal came from Spain with aid he was beaten and beheaded at Metaurus. The Romans forced Hannibal gradually backwards till at last (202 B.C.) they defeated him at Zama Regio in Africa and Carthage submitted (201 B.C.).

Generously put in charge of its government by the Romans, Hannibal maintained his hatred and tried to revive Carthaginian strength for another attack. But the Romans discovered his plan and he fled from one city to another. Cornered in Bythinia (183 B.C.), he took poison.

Explorer of the Bloodstream

WILLIAM
HARVEY

WHAT THE great Aristotle failed to see and Erasistratus, Herophilus, Galen and the 16th Century medical men all fell short of discovering, the patient Englishman, William Harvey, detected and proved: that blood flows steadily from the heart through arteries, veins, lungs and back into the heart.

Educated at Cambridge and the University of Padua, then the foremost medical school of Europe, Harvey, who was born at Folkestone, April 1, 1578, began expounding his circulatory theories in 1616, as a lecturer at the College of Physicians in London. His study and research had been so thorough that he missed only one significant point: the existence of capillary channels to carry blood from arteries to veins. Otherwise, his work was accepted in toto and made possible great strides in medical progress.

Publication of his conclusions on circulation came in 1628. Twenty-three years later his equally painstaking and much longer work on generative processes in animals appeared but, owing to his lack of a microscope, it was much less valuable than the first.

As a practising physician, not too much is known of Harvey, except that he attended King James I and Charles I, as well as other dignitaries. One contemporary disparaged his therapeutic ability. It is known, however, that he performed major surgical operations, such as removal of a breast, and that, on order of the king, he made a post-mortem examination of Thomas Parr, who died in 1635 at the reputed age of 152. There is only one record of his applying his own theories in the care of a patient, when he tied off the arteries supplying blood to a large tumor and thus cured it.

Harvey was appointed warden of Merton College, Oxford, but returned to London when Oxford was surrendered to Parliament in 1646. Being sixty-eight, he retired and lived with one and another of his wealthy brothers, in 1654 declining the honor of election to the presidency of the College of Physicians on account of his age. He died at London, June 3, 1657.

The Little Lion

ALEXANDER

HAMILTON

JUST AS Thomas Jefferson symbolizes the liberal democratic tendencies in American politics, Alexander Hamilton personifies the conservative republican.

He spent his boyhood in the West Indies, where he was born Jan. 11, 1757, on Nevis. At twelve he entered a counting house when his father failed in business, but in 1772 friends sent him to preparatory school in Elizabethtown, N. J., and two years later to King's College, which is now Columbia University.

The Revolutionary War interrupted his studies. He organized an artillery company and quickly made a name for himself in the campaign around New York City in 1776. Promoted in 1777 to lieutenant-colonel, he was for four years Washington's private secretary and confidential aide, resigning for a field command in which he won further acclaim at Yorktown. In 1780 he married Gen. Schuyler's daughter.

Urging a strong central government, he became politically active, serving in the Continental Congress (1782-1783) and the Federal Convention at Philadelphia, where he had an important part in writing the Constitution of the United States. In 1789 President Washington appointed him our first Secretary of the Treasury and he did a heroic job of straightening out the country's tangled finances.

Resigning in 1795 to return to his law practice, he became one of New York's most eminent attorneys. A few years later war with France threatened and Washington made him commander-in-chief of the American army. Fortunately, hostilities were averted. His influence in the government gradually died as he became involved in various political intrigues, one of which led to the famous duel with Aaron Burr.

Burr, angry at Hamilton for the latter's efforts to keep him out of government office, made the challenge and when the two men met at Weehawken, N. J., fatally wounded Hamilton with his first shot. Hamilton died the next day, July 12, 1804.

His political essays, urging a government on the British model, are collected in *The Federalist* and are still much admired.

He Flouted Rome and Built a Church

HENRY VIII

MULTIPLE matrimony, hard-headed politics and religious upheaval were the oddly combined distinguishing marks of this singular monarch's reign. A vigorous, violent, unscrupulous and immensely gifted man, he had an enduring effect on the history, not only of England, but the world.

Born at Greenwich, June 28, 1491, Harry Tudor was the first English king to have a Renaissance education and he became an excellent scholar, linguist and musician, as well as an athlete. Falling heir to the throne April 22, 1509, he lost no time entering his first marriage—with Catharine of Aragon, widow of his brother Arthur, who had died seven years before. The marriage occurred less than two months after his coronation and lasted happily till 1533, when Henry—sure that Catharine could produce no male heirs for the throne—abolished papal jurisdiction over England, secured a divorce and married Anne Boleyn.

Anne was the mother of Elizabeth, later queen, but she had no sons, and in 1536 was beheaded on somewhat flimsy charges of adultery. Henry then married Jane Seymour, who died bearing a son, who later became Edward VI. Ann of Cleves came next, as a gesture toward German Protestants, but was soon divorced and Thomas Cromwell, who arranged this marriage, lost his head. There remained Catharine Howard, executed in 1542, and Catharine Parr, who managed to outlive her spouse.

Henry's break with Rome was necessary to obtain the divorce from Catharine of Aragon, and a male heir was necessary to avoid civil war. But Henry also had his eye on revenue from the monasteries and church lands, and on an increase of the royal power. To gain his end, however, he had to have the support of Parliament, and his measures to win it had the long-term effect of strengthening representative government. Personally, he was no more attached to Protestantism than to Catholicism, and the devious course he pursued between them never made England officially Protestant—that development came under Elizabeth.

Henry's aim was to strengthen and unify England, and to this end he used any brutal and despotic measure that came to his mind. He also laid the foundations of a powerful British navy and played a subtle diplomatic game.

He died Jan. 28, 1547.

"Give Me Liberty or Give Me Death!"

PATRICK
HENRY

N<small>O YOUNG MAN</small> ever gave less promise of becoming a national hero than Patrick Henry. Hunting and fishing, loafing, story-telling and a little fiddle-playing were his only apparent interests. At school he did so poorly that his parents took him out when he was fifteen and put him to work learning a trade. After a year's "training" he went into a small business with his older brother, but this failed within a year, and he was equally unsuccessful later at farming and running a small store.

Somewhere along the line, however, he developed a taste for reading, particularly history, and managed to learn Greek and Latin. He also gained a remarkable understanding of human nature. And at the age of twenty-four, stirred by unprecedented ambition, he took up the study of law. Three years later, in 1763, he acted for the defense in the famous "Parsons' Cause." A two-hour speech held the audience spellbound and so impressed Patrick's hearers with its brilliance that they carried him out of the court-room on their shoulders. From that moment his rank as a leading American orator was assured — and so was his fortune.

But a flourishing legal practice did not satisfy the young Virginian (he was born in Hanover County, May 29, 1736) and in 1765 he found a larger stage for his speaking talents in the House of Burgesses. Here his impassioned speech against the Stamp Act and other British taxes soon made him a leader. In 1774 he was active in the anti-British agitation that led Lord Dunmore to dissolve the House of Burgesses, and a little later he served as a member of the first Revolutionary Convention of Virginia and as a delegate to the first Continental Congress. It was in the Provincial Convention at Richmond that he made the celebrated plea for American resistance that ended with the words, "Give me liberty or give me death!"

Henry was Governor of Virginia from 1776 to 1779 and again from 1784 to 1786. Later he declined offers to be U. S. Senator from Virginia, Secretary of State, Chief Justice of the Supreme Court and special envoy to France. He died June 6, 1799, on his Red Hill, Va., estate.

*European Writer of
American Songs*

VICTOR

HERBERT

Some of the most enduringly popular songs of the United States are the work of this Irish-American composer. *Ah, Sweet Mystery of Life! Kiss Me Again* and *I'm Falling in Love with Someone* are only a few of the many melodies he conceived and made so famous that they are still daily fare on radio and television programs.

Born in Dublin, Ireland, Feb. 1, 1859, Herbert as a youngster showed such musical promise that he was sent to Germany to study. There he worked under a number of the leading teachers and developed his talent so well that he was made the principal violincello player of the orchestra at the Stuttgart court. Later he traveled throughout Europe on concert tours in the unusual role of a soloist with this instrument. Everywhere he was received with enthusiasm.

Word of these successes was not long in reaching New York, then as always avid for new and different talent. In 1886 he was invited by the Metropolitan Orchestra to be its solo violincellist. He accepted and came to the United States, here to spend the rest of his life and become one of America's best-loved song-writers.

A great success with the Metropolitan Orchestra, Herbert soon expanded the field of his efforts. Light opera was his ambition and, though it took some years of working to reach his goal, he did succeed, in 1894, in having his first opera produced. *Prince Ananias* was an immediate success and led to greater things. *The Wizard of the Nile*, produced in 1895, and *The Fortune Teller* (1898) are not so well remembered today, but phonograph recordings of the music of *Babes in Toyland* (1903) still sell well, and *Mademoiselle Modiste* (1905) and *Naughty Marietta* (1910) were unforgettable.

Princess Pat (1915) remains a pleasant memory for everyone who heard it, and *The Red Mill*, first presented in 1906, had a successful revival after World War II. The great Florenz Ziegfeld hired Herbert to do the scores of his *Follies* in 1919, 1921 and 1924. Melodies such as *Sweethearts, Gypsy Love Song* and *Because You're You* have lasted so well in popular taste that they will probably be a permanent feature of American entertainment. Victor Herbert died in New York City, May 26, 1924.

Father of Medicine

HIPPOCRATES

HIPPOCRATES, son of a physician who claimed descent from the Greek God of medicine, Aesculapius, also gave his name to the oath that all doctors take to this day. He was born in 460 B.C., on the island of Cos, which was sacred to Aesculapius.

Despite the strong Greek antipathy towards dissection of the human body, Hippocrates with his astonishing accomplishments in the study of anatomy helped carry his colleagues' knowledge to a new high level. Less conventional for the times was his complete denial of superstition regarding disease. He was convinced that all deterioration of the body followed natural laws and had nothing to do with evil spirits — a conviction which had much to do with the release of medicine for real experiment and discovery.

Hippocrates made two main classifications of the causes of disease: (1) seasonal and climatic, and (2) personal, such as mistakes of diet, lack of exercise and the like. He put more faith in proper eating and well organized regimen than he did in drugs or blood-letting, thus foreshadowing most modern doctors. But in his own practice he did use powerful drugs and leeches.

Hippocrates is supposed to have studied medicine under his father and philosophy under the famed Democritus. He then traveled awhile and returned to practice on his native island of Cos. But modern scholars are certain about very little concerning either his life or his works.

Source of most information regarding Hippocrates, aside from references by contemporaries (two by Plato, one by Artistotle), is the Hippocratic Collection, a group of medical works that began to circulate in the Alexandrian school after 300 B.C. How much of it is truly attributable to Hippocrates, no one knows. But, despite a great deal of error, the Collection has an honest scientific spirit that undoubtedly contributed to the veneration with which Hippocrates has been regarded by members of his profession from the earliest times. One of the most interesting sections of the Collection is "On Wounds of the Head." It contains descriptions of skull operations not greatly differing from those of today.

Hippocrates's age at death has been variously estimated from 85 to 110.

[83]

*Blind Poet
of Ancient Greece*

HOMER

WHAT ARE probably the two greatest poems in European literature may have had no author. The *Iliad* and the *Odyssey* are facts, it has been said, and Homer merely a hypothesis to account for them. Not a thing is definitely known about him.

Herodotus thought Homer lived about 850 B. C., and other scholars placed the date as far back as 1,200 B. C. In ancient Greece itself a tradition regarding him existed and seven cities claimed him as a native — Athens, Argos, Chios, Colophon, Rhodes, Salamis and Smyrna. The tradition had him as a blind poet in his later years, wandering from city to city and earning his bread by singing his verses to the people, accompanying himself on the lyre.

The great German scholar, Friedrich August Wolf, in 1795 presented the idea that the *Iliad* and *Odyssey* were composed and sung in parts by various minstrels (the Homeridae) later the parts being collected by editors and strung together. Wolf claimed that the two classics were certainly not written by one person. After centuries of being chanted and changed by profes-

sional "rhapsodists," they were put roughly in the form we know about 540 by Pisistratus.

Critical study of the Homeric poems began at least as early as the Sixth Century B. C., more or less simultaneously with the beginning of prose writing, and in the next century when the professional teaching of literature started it meant specifically the teaching of Homer. The "rhapsodists" had audiences numbering thousands for their recitals of the *Iliad* and *Odyssey*. Cultured Greeks sometimes knew the long poems by heart.

The most authoritative early work of editing the confused Homeric papyri was done by Aristarchus of Samothrace, head of the Alexandrian library. About 150 B. C. he published two editions of the poems that very closely conformed to what we read today.

Homer has been translated into virtually all civilized languages, the most famous versions in English verse being by Cowper and Pope. But the difficulty of presenting Homer's rhythm and flavor in English verse make a prose translation more valuable.

Artist of the Sea and Soil

WINSLOW
HOMER

WINSLOW HOMER, though he studied in Paris briefly, was very little influenced by European schools in his painting. Both his subject matter and his approach were American.

A Bostonian, he was born Feb. 24, 1836, and after his school days were over went to work as apprentice for a lithographer. He was nineteen then and two years later he had opened his own studio in Boston, specializing in drawings for wood-engravings.

He moved to New York in 1859 and studied art at the night school of National Academy of Design. By the time the Civil War started he was ready to do sketches for *Harper's Weekly* and did them from the front lines. Some of his more enduring work also stemmed from the war — *Home, Sweet Home*, for example, which was one of the two first paintings he exhibited in 1863. And *Prisoners from the Front* — his most popular painting — was another war product.

Some of his other well known oil paintings are *Snap the Whip, Eating Water-melon, The Cotton Pickers, Visit from the Old Mistress, Sunday Morning, The Life-Line* and *The Coming of the Gale.*

Despite the fame of his oils, Homer's real reputation is for water colors — *genre* pictures, chiefly, marked by rugged strength and a fresh originality rather than technical skill or any special line or color technique. Best known are the marines painted at Gloucester, Mass., and such other works as *Inside the Bar, The Voice from the Cliffs, Tynemouth, Wrecking of a Vessel* and *Lost on the Grand Banks.* There were a few English subjects and scenes among these, *The Voice from the Cliffs* for example, but his real interest was America — Union soldiers, Negro farmers, rough New England seas and Gloucester fishermen. From 1884 on he lived at Scarboro, Maine, and there painted such notable pictures as *Maine Coast, Cannon Rock* and *Northeaster.* He died in 1910.

Homer was a member of the Society of Painters in Water Color of New York and the National Academy of Design.

"Mine Eyes Have Seen the Glory"

JULIA WARD
HOWE

Considering all the tireless work in good causes that Julia Ward Howe did in her time, one is forced to feel the irony of the fact that she is remembered almost entirely for a single poem published in the *Atlantic Monthly*. *The Battle Hymn of the Republic* was a stirring and widely popular piece of versification, during the Civil War and afterwards, but Mrs. Howe not only wrote other good poetry, she was also an energetic and effective proponent of all the important liberal theories of her time.

A native New Yorker, she was born on Manhattan Island May 27, 1819. From childhood she wrote poetry, most of it being published in 1898 in a volume called *From Sunset Ridge: Poems Old and New.* She married a Bostonian, Samuel Gridley Howe, of equally humanitarian spirit, who served as a soldier and surgeon in the Greek war for independence from Turkey and afterwards labored at home for prison reform, better care of the feeble-minded and abolition of such anachronisms as imprisonment for debt and human slavery. Her own crusades coincided with some of his, but most had a wider aim.

Mrs. Howe was an ardent advocate of women's suffrage long before the topic came into the area of serious political discussion, and a vigorous defender of her sex's rights in other directions. She wrote and lectured on German philosophy, helped her husband edit the *Commonwealth*, preached now and then from Unitarian pulpits and was the author of a number of books. The biographical ones, *A Memoir of Dr. Samuel G. Howe*, published in the year of his death, 1876, *Margaret Fuller* (1883), *Sketches of Representative Women of New England* (1905) and her own *Reminiscences* (1899), retain the most interest today. Her travel books, essays and experiments in drama were less successful.

In the cause of abolition she lectured and wrote assiduously, as she did for prison reform. World peace was another of her dominant interests. And she gave herself unstintingly to many other high-minded purposes.

Julia Ward Howe died at her summer home, Oak Glen, R. I., Oct. 17, 1910.

[86]

Explorer
of the Northern Seas

HENRY
HUDSON

Except for the years 1607 to 1611, nothing is known about this bold English sailor. There is no record of his birth or early life and even the fact of his death is uncertain.

He first appears in history as captain of a tiny English ship, the *Hopeful,* on which he and a handful of men in 1607 set out to find the fabled Northwest Passage. They sailed along the coasts of Greenland and Spitzbergen, but could not penetrate the great ice barrier to the north and returned to England after a four months' cruise.

On his second voyage, the next year, Hudson sailed northeastward and reached Nova Zembla. His third, in 1609, was made for the Dutch East India Company in the Half Moon with twenty men. Sailing from Amsterdam, he again made Nova Zembla, hoping to cross the Kara Sea and reach the Pacific Ocean. But his men became mutinous over the extreme cold and he turned about, heading westward across the Atlantic for Davis Strait, where explorers of the New World thought there was only a narrow strip of land separating the two oceans. Accidentally perhaps, he sailed south of his destination and reached the Nova Scotia shore, afterwards going south as far as latitude 35°. Reversing his course again, he entered the Hudson River and sailed up it to the site of Albany before deciding that this was not the way to India.

Hudson set out again in April, 1610, this time employed by a British company. His *Discovery* reached Greenland in June and he sailed on through the strait now named for him to the huge inland sea called Hudson Bay. After months of exploring he decided to remain for the winter and go on in the spring. In November ice confirmed his decision by locking the ship in, but his hungry and quarrelsome men mutinied when spring set the *Discovery* free. They put Hudson, his son, the loyal men and a few sick ones in a small boat and sailed away. This occurred in June, 1611, and is the last that is known about Hudson.

Hudson's voyages made no really new discoveries, but they did encourage the development of rich fisheries at Spitzbergen and the great fur industry of Hudson Bay.

[87]

As a Politician, Foolish,
As a Novelist, Famous
As a Poet, Great.

VICTOR
HUGO

A CYNIC, asked the name of the greatest 19th Century French poet, replied: "Unfortunately, Victor Hugo." Widely known as are such novels as *Les Miserables*, it was his verse that had the most powerful literary influence, affecting such different poets as Verlaine, Baudelaire and Rimbaud. Politically, although he had ambition and held office, he was inept and so ranting oratorically that in the end he could not even obtain a hearing in the National Assembly of which he was a member. Personally, he was an opportunist and a shrewd one. Hardly a noble character, he explained his notorious, fifty-year-long affair with Juliette Drouet by the statement that he was "redeeming" her.

Few famous lives are divided into as many "periods" as that of Hugo. No less than seven distinct eras comprised his career, which began at Besançon, Feb. 26, 1802. Even the earliest childhood period was important for the excitement of following his father, a Napoleonic general, in the Italian and Spanish campaigns, and for the effect of his parents' dislike of each other on his own personality. Then he had an "infant prodigy" period, from the age of thirteen to twenty, when an Academy poetry prize brought him the name "sublime baby" from Chateaubriand. Next he had a Royalist phase, during which he deliberately curried favor with verses directed at the court. When French readers seemed ready for the literary "romantic revolution," he made himself its leader and had a crusading period. From 1830 to 1845 the theme was success, in novels, poetry and drama. Then, after concentration on politics, came the exile of 1851, when Napoleon III became dictator; it lasted eighteen years, on the island of Guernsey, and Hugo is said to have reveled in every moment of his martyrdom. In 1870, on reëstablishment of the Republic, he returned to Paris for the final fifteen-year period of triumph, when his literary fame was universal and popular idolatry so great that on his eightieth birthday 600,000 persons acclaimed him. By now he had the sense to keep away from the French Senate, of which he was a member.

A supreme master of language and meter, Hugo is considered by present-day critics to have lacked the character and high intellect necessary for a writer of immortal rank. But in his time he was a literary power not to be deprecated. He died May 22, 1885, two years after Juliette, who was faithful to the end.

[88]

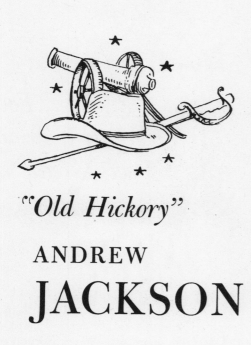

"Old Hickory"

ANDREW

JACKSON

As a soldier, Jackson was precocious: his first battle with the British (Hanging Rock in 1780) coming when he was only thirteen. As a man, he was pugnacious and fought a number of duels, killing one antagonist and being himself severely wounded several times. As a politician and statesman, he left an indelible mark in American history, establishing the political power of the common man, reducing excessive States' Rights, and paying off the national debt.

A wild, quick-tempered youth, born March 15, 1767, at Waxhaw, S. C., Jackson had little education. Nevertheless, he was admitted to the bar at the age of twenty and before the turn of the century served as a judge, Congressman and U. S. Senator. He became a national hero in the War of 1812, when he repulsed the English at New Orleans, Jan. 9, 1815, with a loss of their commander and 2,000 men, while he lost eight. This saved the Mississippi for the United States.

He ran in 1824 for the Presidency, winning the greatest number of electoral votes, but not a majority. When the House of Representatives chose John Quincy Adams for President, Jackson felt he and the people had been defrauded, and organized an opposition so vigorous that he was easily victor in the 1828 election.

During his two administrations Jackson replaced so many officeholders that the so-called "spoils system" is considered to have stemmed from his time. He also had the first "kitchen cabinet," a group of personal friends on whom he relied for advice rather than on the formally appointed Cabinet. In general, the effect of his Presidency was to democratize American government, but his firm action against South Carolina's effort to nullify the tariff law had the result of strengthening the Federal Government in its relations with the States.

After his two terms Jackson lived in retirement except for activities in support of the slavery cause. He died at Nashville, June 8, 1845.

The Carpenter
Who Was Christ,
the Redeemer

JESUS

Lɪᴛᴛʟᴇ is known of the life of the Nazarene who became the founder of the Christian religion beyond what is given in the four Gospels of the New Testament and a few additional writings such as the letters of Paul. According to these Gospels Jesus is represented as being born of a virgin named Mary and of Joseph, a carpenter, a descendant of the house of David. Historians set the date of the child's birth at somewhere between the years 8 and 4 B.C., and the place at Bethlehem.

Jesus was thirty years old when John the Baptist (son of Elizabeth, cousin of Mary) began preaching, "The Kingdom of Heaven is at hand, repent." Vast crowds gathered to hear the gaunt preacher's prophetic voice and to be baptized in the Jordan. Among the listeners was the young carpenter of Nazareth, who offered Himself to a reluctant John for baptism.

The die was cast. Convinced of His divine calling, Jesus began to gather about Him a little group, the twelve Disciples, who recognized in Him the future leader of His nation, the Son of God. And so began those few crowded years of His ministry during which He went about the sorely distressed land of Palestine spreading the gospel of love and hope. The ruling classes, including the priests of the old religion, distrusted the fundamental democracy of the teachings of Jesus and His calm assertion that He and His Father were one. Eventually, when they saw the impression His teachings and healings were having on the people, they realized that it was necessary to put Jesus to death.

His death came about when He and His Disciples went into Jerusalem to observe the Passover. Every Christian is familiar with the events of the next few days, of the Last Supper with the Disciples, the betrayal of Judas Iscariot, the arrest of Jesus after the bitter night on Gethsemane, of His trial before Caoaphas and the Sanhedrin, His appearance before the vacillating Pilate, His crucifixion and burial and resurrection and final ascension by which He became the founder of the Church and the dominating personality of the Christian era.

Father of Democracy

THOMAS

JEFFERSON

ONE OF THE three or four greatest American Presidents, Thomas Jefferson was also an architect, a scientific farmer, a writer, a lawyer, a mathematician, an inventor, a musician, an accomplished linguist and founder of the University of Virginia. Despite these impressive practical achievements, his deepest significance to Americans is probably as a personification of the liberal democratic ideal.

A Virginian of good family, born at Shadwell April 13, 1743, Jefferson loved horses and outdoor sports, as well as singing and dancing, but refused to gamble or play cards, to smoke tobacco or engage in a personal quarrel. After studying at William and Mary College he practised law and entered politics, first as a justice of the peace, then as a member of the Virginia House of Burgesses and of the Continental Congress. He was, of course, the author of the Declaration of Independence.

A term as governor of Virginia (1779-1781) preceded his return to Congress in 1783, when he headed the committee considering the treaty of peace with England and persuaded his native state to cede the territory northwest of the Ohio River to the United States. His resolution that slavery should be outlawed there was rejected in 1784 but passed in 1787. In 1785 he succeeded Benjamin Franklin as minister to France and then became Secretary of State. It was in this office that the fundamental political differences between him and Alexander Hamilton crystallized into the formation of the Democratic and Federalist parties.

Jefferson was elected Vice-President in 1796 and four years later tied with Aaron Burr in electoral votes for the Presidency. Hamilton's influence in the House of Representatives won for Jefferson. His two terms in the White House were marked by the Louisiana Purchase, which doubled United States territory, the Lewis and Clark expedition, and his love of simplicity and distaste for pomp and ceremony, which had a pronounced effect on Washington manners.

Refusing a third term, he retired to his Monticello estate and gave the rest of his life to writing, scientific pursuits, farming, music, reading and correspondence. He died July 4, 1826.

America's
First Naval Hero

JOHN PAUL
JONES

THIS INTREPID American seaman, born in Scotland in 1747 as plain John Paul, performed such magnificent exploits that he fired his adopted country's imagination during the Revolutionary War, setting an example of valor that is still an inspiration to the Navy.

John Paul went to sea at the age of ten, making one of his first voyages to Virginia. The slave trade with which so much shipping was then occupied disgusted him and at the age of twenty-one he resigned his job to return to England. En route the captain and first mate died, and he brought the ship to port, whereupon its owners made him master.

In 1773 he inherited a brother's estate in Virginia, settling there for a time and adopting the surname of Jones for reasons that are not at all clear. When the Revolution broke out he went on a successful expedition against New Providence in the Bahamas. In May of 1776 he got command of the *Providence*, convoying supplies to New York, and in August a captain's commission. Cruising between Nova Scotia and Bermuda, in one seven weeks' period besides sinking eight vessels, he captured six brigantines, one ship and one sloop.

The next year he won command of the new *Ranger* and crossed the Atlantic with dispatches for the American commissioners in France. After their delivery he made a sensational attack on the British port of Whitehaven, spiking the guns of the two protecting forts and unsuccessfully trying to burn the ships in the harbor.

An abortive effort to attack the Scottish port of Leith preceded his most famous sea battle. Returning from Leith to France in a refitted old French ship, the *Bon Homme Richard,* Jones met the powerful British man-of-war, *Serapis*, and in a furious three-and-a-half-hour engagement, during which the two ships were lashed together and the *Bon Homme Richard* received damage that sank her two days later, the Americans forced the British to surrender.

In 1781 Jones was awarded a gold medal by Congress. In 1788 came an offer from Catherine the Great to fight the Turks, but jealousies among Russian officers decided him to resign and he settled in Paris, where he died in 1792. In 1905 his body was reburied at Annapolis, with naval honors.

"O Rare Ben Jonson!"

BEN
JONSON

Intimate friends of Shakespeare, front-rank dramatist in his own right, poet, masque and prose writer, soldier, bricklayer and eminent scholar, Ben Jonson was one of the brightest lights of the Elizabethan age.

Westminster-born, probably in 1573, Jonson said he was "poorly brought up" and it is true that he did work in his step-father's brickyard. But it is also true that he went to an excellent school under the erudite William Camden, where he was thoroughly grounded in the classics. From the brickyard he ran away to fight with English troops against the Spanish in the Netherlands, and reached London about 1592.

Five years later he came to notice as a player and hack playwright at the Fortune Theatre. His ability as an actor apparently was nothing phenomenal, though he could teach other actors, but in 1598 his comedy, *Every Man in His Humor*, won him his first triumph as a writer. Shakespeare is said to have played in the cast.

That same year Jonson killed an actor, Gabriel Spencer, in a duel and went to prison, barely escaping the gallows. Under Elizabeth the Catholic faith was heresy, but Jonson in jail increased his risks by embracing it. Nevertheless, he won freedom and soon afterwards wrote another successful comedy, *Every Man Out of His Humor*. His first tragedy, *Sejanus*, came in 1603.

Under James I he swiftly adapted himself to writing court entertainments and masques, which later he dignified to the point of being true literature. He also continued with his comedies, producing *Volpone, or the Fox* in 1605, *Epicoene, or The Silent Woman* in 1609, and *Bartholomew Fair* in 1614. And he wrote many songs, the best remembered being *Drink to Me Only with Thine Eyes*. In 1613 he traveled on the Continent with Sir Walter Raleigh's son, later writing a description of the Punic Wars for the senior Raleigh's *History of the World*.

All his life a hard-drinking, hard-working man, Jonson in old age was ill and impoverished. He died Aug. 6, 1637, and over his grave a stonecutter, not understanding the Latin inscription intended for him ("*Orare* Ben Jonson," meaning "Pray for Ben Jonson"), left a better epitaph: "O rare Ben Jonson."

Maid of Orleans

JOAN OF ARC

THE MYSTIC fascination this little peasant girl exerted on the French soldiery of her time continues down the centuries to hold the imagination of writers, readers and playgoers.

Daughter of a common laborer, Joan was born in the village of Domrémy sometime in the year 1412. Wholly uneducated, she had a dreamy, visionary nature that was peculiarly susceptible to the superstitious tales of the ignorant countryside. Supernatural forces were as natural to her childhood as the hard realities of existence, and she made little if any effort to distinguish between them.

Conscious of the distress invading English soldiers were causing her fellow Frenchmen, she listened dutifully to the spiritual voices calling on her to go to the aid of the Dauphin. Charges of insanity and lying made obstacles, but she persevered and at last achieved an audience with the king's eldest son. Impressed with her religious ardor and perhaps also with the practical effects it might have on his fortunes, the Dauphin bade her lead his troops.

With sword and white banner and in a man's uniform, the Maid on April 29, 1428, led 10,000 Frenchmen into the besieged city of Orleans. How much was intuitive military skill and how much quiet direction from older hands is hard to say now, but she quickly made a series of such successful raids against the British that they raised the seige. Her victory put sudden and electric spirit into the Dauphin's whole army, and demoralized the equally superstitious English soldiers. Soon Joan was able to conduct the Dauphin to Rheims, where he was crowned Charles VII.

In May, 1430, however, attempting to relieve the besieged town of Compiegne, she was captured. After a long, shameful trial, in which Charles showed an ungrateful lack of interest, she was condemned by the Bishop of Beauvais as a sorceress and burned at the stake May 30, 1431, in the public street of Rouen.

In 1456 the government reviewed her trial and declared her innocent. In 1920 Pope Benedict XV canonized her a saint.

Germ Detective

ROBERT

KOCH

WITH a microscope that his thrifty wife is said to have bought with money saved on groceries, Robert Koch began a career in bacteriology that has few if any parallels.

Born at Klausthal in the German province of Hanover, Dec. 11, 1843, he studied medicine at the University of Göttingen and practised in several German towns before settling at Wollstein. It was here, in 1876, that he succeeded in making a pure culture of the anthrax bacillus, a germ that most often attacks animals, but sometimes human beings as well. Publication of this work brought him fame in scientific circles and in 1880 he was appointed to the Imperial Health Board in Berlin, where he was able to give more time to research.

His ingenuity and patience in devising new methods of bacteriological investigation enabled him, as early as 1882, to isolate and make visible the bacillus of tuberculosis—a discovery that gave great impetus to other scientific research. In 1883 he announced a preventive method of inoculation against anthrax. The same year he headed a group of distinguished scientists sent by the German government to study cholera in India and Egypt, and was largely responsible for their success in indentifying the germ of this disease.

About 1890 Koch developed a substance from tubercle bacilli, which it was hoped would cure the "white plague." The bacteriologist himself made no exaggerated claims, but rumor built up great excitement and it was a heavy disappointment when the tuberculin proved to be much more helpful in diagnosis than in treatment.

Between 1896 and 1906 he visited Africa several times, searching for the cause of malaria, cattle plague and sleeping sickness. He demonstrated finally that some species of the African tsetse fly at the moment of biting transmit the germ of sleeping sickness to human beings.

Among many other honors, Koch in 1905 received the Nobel prize for medicine. He published many valuable works on bacteriology, his last article, *The Epidemiology of Tuberculosis*, being read before the Berlin Academy of Sciences just six weeks before his death, which occurred April 7, 1910, at Baden-Baden.

Greatest of the
Mongol Emperors

KUBLAI KHAN

In more distant military ventures Kublai was less fortunate. Several expeditions against Japan ended in disaster, and wars with Cochin China and Java also went against him. An attack on Burma, however, was more successful, the Mongol armies overrunning the country as far as the Irawaddy delta. In peaceful missions to other nations the Emperor usually had good luck, gaining professions of homage from southern India, eastern Africa and Madagascar.

A motley army of Asians fought Kublai's battles and in his entourage he had adventurers, scientists, governors and diplomats from everywhere. Marco Polo is the best remembered of the group, and from him we know of Kublai Khan. One of the things he tells is that Kublai tried to get European priests to teach his people, and, failing, turned to Tibetan Buddhism. Marco Polo also tells of Kublai's splendid court, with its lavish entertainments, of magnificent hunting parties, and the intricate system of tax agents necessary to collect money to pay for them. Despite his good nature and essentially intellectual inclination, the Emperor was so extravagant, both in personal and military expenses, that his people were often close to rebellion over the cost. Kublai died in 1294, at the age of seventy-eight.

GRANDSON of the warrior Jenghiz Khan, but a benevolent intellectual himself, despite his conquests, Kublai Khan became the acknowledged ruler of more human beings than any previous man in history. When the half-century of Mongol campaigning in China ended (1279), Kublai held at least nominal sovereignty clear to the frontiers of Poland. For the first time he made the name of a Chinese emperor familiar to Europeans.

At the age of ten he took part in Jenghiz's last campaign (1226-1227) and legend has it that the old soldier took note on his deathbed of young Kublai's ability. He did not come to the Mongol throne until 1259 and even then had to fight his brother, Arikbugha, and his cousin, Kaidu, for the disputed title. Winning, he went on to establish his new capital (1264) at Peking and to complete the conquest of south China.

French Ambassador of Liberty

LAFAYETTE

THE ROMANTIC figure of Lafayette is an enduring symbol of the democratic friendship between France and the United States.

His father died when he was two and his mother when he was thirteen, leaving him the title of marquis and a handsome fortune. Three years later he married and began his military career, as a captain of dragoons.

At the outbreak of the American Revolution Lafayette made up his mind to help the Colonists. Although the French king forbade it, he fitted out a ship, escaped from a Spanish port and reached Georgetown, S. C., in April of 1777. He had with him only eleven supporters. Nevertheless, their arrival lifted the Colonists' flagging spirits. Lafayette offered to serve as a simple volunteer, but Congress, on July 31, commissioned him a major-general and he soon became a member of Washington's staff, also a life-long friend of the General's.

In his first action, at Brandywine (Sept. 11, 1777), he was wounded. That same fall he received command of a division and in the spring distinguished himself at Barren Hill. Later, at Monmouth and Yorktown, he added further laurels to his crown, receiving thanks from Congress and Gen. Washington. Meanwhile, when England declared war on France, he went home and returned with both sea and land forces to help the American cause.

After Cornwallis's surrender, Lafayette was made a major-general in the French army and continued to fight the battle of freedom during the French Revolution. A constitutional monarchist, he worked in the National Assembly for such liberal causes as religious tolerance, popular representation, emancipation of slaves, freedom of the press and abolition of noble titles. Declining command of the National Guard in 1790. he later took active part in the war with Austria and Prussia. Then his attempts to restore the monarchy brought him five years' imprisonment, ending with release by Napoleon in 1797.

On two post-war visits to the United States he was received with lavish honors, Congress in 1824 awarding him a gift of $200,000. He died at Paris, May 20, 1834.

Father of the

Russian Revolution

NIKOLAI
LENIN

To THIS simple-living, hard-working lawyer belongs credit, more than to any other one man, for creation of the mighty power that is Soviet Russia today.

He was born at Simbirsk (now Ulyanovsk) April 22, 1870, son of a teacher. In his first year at the Kazan University law school he was banished to Siberia for taking part in student politics. Returning in 1889, he added Karl Marx to his studies and became a leader of the radical Social Democrats. For three years, beginning in 1891, he practised law at Samara, then went to St. Petersburg to concentrate on the propaganda work that was to be his real career.

Another period of imprisonment and exile lasted from December of 1895 to early 1900. During it he wrote most of *Development of Capitalism in Russia,* and afterwards went to Switzerland to edit a revolutionary paper. In 1905 the Russo-Japanese War gave rise to the unsuccessful revolt at Moscow, from which Lenin, along with many colleagues, had to flee the country. From this experience he formulated the three policies that eventually culminated in the true Revolution: (1) temporary seizure by the people of political freedom, (2) creation of revolutionary power in soviets of workers, soldiers and peasants and (3) use of force against oppressors of the people.

Urging these policies and working for an international Communist party, Lenin remained outside Russia till the uprising of February, 1917, when he returned to Petrograd. During the Kerensky regime his activities were necessarily of the underground variety, but they bore fruit and the Bolshevists soon had control, Lenin becoming head of the Soviet of People's Commissaries and establishing the dictatorship of the proletariat, with the new government transferred to Moscow.

Wounded in 1918 by a political opponent, he quickly recovered and successfully brought the infant state through foreign intervention, counter-revolution and diplomatic non-recognition by other powers. Before he fell ill in 1921 Soviet Russia had a firm political foundation and was ready for the years of intense economic development that lay ahead. Lenin died Jan. 21, 1924, his body being enshrined in the Kremlin.

Leader of a Lost Cause

ROBERT E.
LEE

Of all the magnificent soldiers who fought in the American Civil War, Lee was greatest in military skill and best loved by his men.

Son of the famous "Lighthorse Harry" Lee, cavalry hero of the Revolution, Robert Edward Lee was born at Stratford, Va., Jan. 19, 1807. He was graduated second in the class of 1829 at West Point and made his first military reputation during the Mexican War, after which the commanding general, Winfield Scott, called him "the greatest living soldier in America."

From 1852 to 1855 he was commander of West Point, making many improvements in the Academy's course of instruction. From there he went to Texas, where he served as a cavalry officer till the capture of the arsenal at Harper's Ferry by John Brown. Lee commanded the troops that put down this insurrection.

In 1861, President Lincoln offered command of the Army of the United States to Lee, but the latter declined, though he personally opposed secession. When Virginia joined the Confederate States, Lee resigned his commission. In early 1862 he became military adviser to Jefferson Davis. Then he succeeded Johnston as supreme commander and against McClellan's vastly bigger army organized the brilliant defense of Richmond that ended in complete defeat for the Union forces. Lee went on to invade Maryland, winning the second battle of Bull Run and Antietam. In 1863 he again penetrated Northern territory, but this time was repulsed at Gettysburg. The following year Grant became commander of the Union Army and began his relentless march on Richmond. Lee's defense was brilliant as always and costly to the North, but in the end he had to capitulate to superior strength, surrendering on April 9, 1865.

After the war he served as president of Washington College (now Washington and Lee University) till his death on Oct. 12, 1870. His wife, Mary Custis, great-granddaughter of Martha Washington, outlived him by three years.

Lee's military tactics were much in advance of his time and have provided profitable study ever since in war schools all over the world.

The Great Emancipator

ABRAHAM

LINCOLN

THE STORY of Lincoln is a great favorite with Americans. His fence-splitting, unschooled youth; his trip by flat-boat down the Mississippi to New Orleans, where the sight of a slave market left an indelible mark on his memory; his years as a lawyer, with all the wonderful anecdotes proving his droll humor and courtroom sagacity; the terrible, testing term of his Presidency, when the country he loved was split in bloody fragments; and then the final senseless tragedy of his assassination just five days after Lee's surrender at Appomattox — all these are well remembered things.

Lincoln was born in Hardin County, Ky., Feb. 12, 1809, and moved to Indiana, where his mother died, in 1816. He had no more than a year's formal education, but was always an omnivorous reader. He clerked in a store in Illinois, became a village postmaster and worked as a surveyor before beginning to practise law in Springfield in 1839. Elected to Congress in 1846, he served one not very successful term and did not seem a likely candidate for high political

honors until the debates with Senator Stephen A. Douglas over slavery in 1858. Lincoln's anti-slavery speeches finally won him the Republican nomination for the Presidency in 1860. With the Democrats split, his election was insured.

The long struggle between North and South over the question of slavery promptly culminated in one of the bloodiest wars of history. Early defeats in the field combined with political difficulties and a melancholy family life to make his situation agonizing. But iron courage and a great wisdom carried him through.

Beyond a doubt, the mad plot in which John Wilkes Booth shot the President at Ford's Theatre (April 14, 1865) made Reconstruction for the South a more painful process than it needed to be, for Lincoln would surely have found better policies than those of his successor.

One of his enduring claims to fame was as a writer. In a day of florid oratory, his speeches (the Gettysburg address, for a sample) stood out with beautiful clarity, simplicity and logic.

Weaver of Lyrical Legends

HENRY WADSWORTH
LONGFELLOW

LONGFELLOW was far and away the most popular American poet of his time. While not considered an immortal, in the sense of Shakespeare and Dante, he is still very widely read.

He was born at Portland, Maine, Feb. 27, 1807, son of a well-to-do lawyer, and graduated from Bowdoin College. Appointment to be professor of modern languages at Bowdoin carried with it a training period abroad and Longfellow, immediately after graduation, spent three years in France, Italy, Spain and Germany studying their languages. *Outre Mer*, a collection of sketches in the Washington Irving manner, recorded his experiences; it was published in 1835.

In 1834 he was made professor of modern languages at Harvard, the transfer again carrying with it a sojourn abroad, this time in England, Sweden and Denmark. He taught at Harvard for eighteen years, simultaneously writing the verses which made him famous. *Voices of the Night*, his first success, was published in 1839. *Ballads* appeared in 1841, with such well remembered short poems as *The Wreck of the Hesperus*, *Excelsior* and *The Village Blacksmith*.

His first wife having died in 1835, Longfellow married a second time in 1843. His bride, Frances Appleton, had been the heroine of his prose romance, *Hyperion*, and when she was accidentally burned to death in 1861 gave inspiration for one of his most deeply emotional poems, *Cross of Snow*, which he did not print, considering it too personal.

He resigned from Harvard in 1854 to concentrate on writing. Of his longer poems, *Evangeline* had already appeared, in 1847. *Hiawatha* came in 1855 and three years later *The Courtship of Miles Standish*. There were also numerous volumes of shorter poems and a record of his European studies, *The Poets and Poetry of Europe*, which was published in 1845. His two most ambitious works were a translation of Dante's *Divine Comedy* and a trilogy called *Christus*, on both of which he worked for years.

A kindly, generous man who gave much time to autograph-hunters and uninvited callers, Longfellow lived in the Craigie House at Cambridge till March 24, 1882, when he died.

[101]

The Great Reformer

MARTIN

LUTHER

Before he was thirty this young German priest defied the entire hierarchy of the Roman Catholic Church and in so doing laid the groundwork for the Protestant Reformation that swept over much of Europe.

The son of a miner, Martin Luther was born Nov. 10, 1483, at Eisleben, Germany. Educated at schools in Magdeburg and Eisenach and graduated from the University of Erfurt in 1501, he entered the Augustinian monastery at Erfurt and became a Catholic priest in 1507. As a preacher he was an immediate success and his eloquence served him well also in teaching philosophy at the University of Wittenberg and theology at Erfurt.

A journey to Rome in 1511 woke him to malpractices then current in the religious world, particularly the shameless traffic in indulgences —openly sold remissions of sin. On his return he drew up ninety-five theses questioning the Pope's right to forgive sins and pinned them to the door of the Wittenberg Cathedral. It was the first public protest against the indulgence trade, though there had been plenty of private objection, and it caused a great furore.

When Luther refused the local Church's demand that he recant, the Pope summoned him to Rome, but the Elector of Saxony offered protection and Luther stood his ground. In fact, he grew bolder. In a series of three pamphlets he attacked the whole papal system, upholding the right of each individual to interpret the Bible for himself. For just such views John Huss had been executed a century before. The Pope's threat of excommunication, which promptly followed, was burned by Luther before a Wittenberg crowd.

At the famous Diet of Worms Luther again refused to recant and was put under the ban of the Empire. Nevertheless, his ideas spread and by 1530 had won all of Germany to the Reformation. Luther himself made translations of the New and Old Testaments, set up a new form of church service and government as a model in Wittenberg, and married an ex-nun, who bore him six children. In 1540 he figured in the new church's first scandal, by sanctioning the bigamous marriage of Philip of Hesse. He died Feb. 18, 1546, at his birthplace, Eisleben.

"I Will Return!"

GEN. DOUGLAS
MacARTHUR

Few commanders in World War II had more dramatic experiences than Gen. MacArthur. Completely defeated in the surprise Japanese attack of December, 1941, he escaped the Philippines by submarine with the promise: "I will return." Two and a half years later he did return, this time heading the mightiest military force the East has ever seen, and swept the enemy from the Islands.

Douglas MacArthur was born Jan. 26, 1880, at Little Rock, Ark., son of an Army Chief of Staff who had also served in the Philippines. He had a brilliant record at West Point and served during World War I with great distinction as commander of the famous Rainbow Division. Afterwards he was made superintendent of the Academy at West Point.

Following tours of duty in the Philippines, he was in 1930 appointed Chief of Staff at Washington, like his father. But reappointment in 1934 broke all military precedents. In 1935 he went back to the Philippines as Field Marshal of President Quezon's new Philippine Army, retiring in 1937 from the American Army and being recalled in 1941 to head U. S. forces in the Far East when the Japanese began to threaten.

After the débacle on Bataan, the Japanese swiftly overran most of the Orient and the Allied problem was chiefly to keep a foothold from which to launch a counterattack, when men and equipment became available. MacArthur first expected to have to defend Australia, but the victories at Guadalcanal and the Coral Sea permitted him to hang on to the southern tip of New Guinea. Later his enveloping "island-hopping" policy, with the help of air and naval superiority, greatly speeded victory in the Pacific. With no navy or air force left after the Philippine campaign and the awful fact of the atomic bomb demonstrated at Hiroshima and Nagasaki, the Japanese collapsed in August, 1945, and accepted MacArthur as their Occupation Commander with a veneration previously accorded only to an Emperor.

Like Gen. Eisenhower, MacArthur was mentioned as a possible Presidential candidate in 1948, but had insufficient support.

The Man Who Made the Supreme Court Supreme

JOHN
MARSHALL

THE astonishing legal genius and personal force of John Marshall made the Supreme Court not only an equal, but at most times a prevailing power in the tripartite system of checks and balances that is the United States Government. Andrew Jackson could say, "Marshall has made his decision, now let him enforce it," but in the long run Marshall's decisions enforced themselves—by strength of logic, by their inherent necessity for progress, and by the cumulative authority of the Court.

One of the many great Virginians in American history, Marshall was born Sept. 24, 1755, in what later became Fauquier County. He fought in the Revolution, studied law briefly and in 1786 tried a case, Hite vs. Fairfax, which, when he won, made him leader of the Virginia bar. After declining offers from President Washington to be attorney-general (1795) and minister to France (1796), he was elected to the House of Representatives in 1799, made Secretary of State in 1800 and appointed Chief Justice of the Supreme Court Jan. 31, 1801.

Under John Jay, first Chief Justice, the Court had lagged behind the Executive and the Congress in influence. Under Marshall, it flourished.

By his simply worded, beautifully logical decisions he established the Supreme Court's power to interpret the Constitution. He also established the Federal Government's right to do many things necessary for the welfare of the country, such as controlling interstate commerce.

Most dramatic and revealing of all Marshall's trials was that of Aaron Burr for treason. A member of the Federalist party, the Chief Justice had been a close friend of Alexander Hamilton, whom Burr killed in the famous duel at Weehawken. When Burr made his ill-starred expedition down the Mississippi, President Jefferson mishandled public announcements and let the whole American people become inflamed against Burr. But the law and the evidence were clear to Marshall, and he could not be prejudiced or intimidated. Burr went free, no matter how guilty his ambitions were, because there was no proof of guilt in his acts.

Marshall suffered injuries in a stagecoach accident early in 1835 and died July 6 of that year, at Philadelphia.

For Her Two Thrones— But not the One She Sought

MARY
QUEEN OF SCOTS

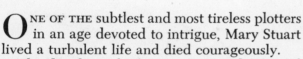

ONE OF THE subtlest and most tireless plotters in an age devoted to intrigue, Mary Stuart lived a turbulent life and died courageously.

The daughter of King James V and Mary of Lorraine, she was born in Scotland in December, 1542, and with the death of her father became queen a few days later. When she was a year old a marriage with Edward, son of Henry VIII, was arranged, but the Scottish Parliament refused to sanction it and war with England resulted. To resist Henry's invasions the Scots renewed the old alliance with France and Mary was betrothed to the Dauphin Francis. She moved to France in 1548, married Francis ten years later and returned in 1561, after his death, to Scotland.

Mary wanted Elizabeth, now Queen of England, to accept her claim to the English throne if the virgin monarch died childless and Elizabeth's threat to withhold such acceptance stopped Mary from marrying a Habsburg prince. In 1565 her second marriage took place, with Lord Darnley, who had a claim to both the island crowns.. When this foolish young man

conspired in the murder of her favorite, Rizzio, he signed his own death warrant. In 1567 an explosion wrecked the building where he was supposed to sleep and he was found the next day strangled.

Three months later Bothwell, who was Darnley's actual murderer, became Mary's third husband. The Scottish lords immediately rose and at Carberry Hill showed themselves so superior to the Queen's forces that she was surrendered without a battle. Abdicating in favor of her son, James, she was imprisoned at Lochleven, but escaped for one more battle, at Langside. Defeated again, she threw herself on Elizabeth's protection. This was in 1568.

For the next nineteen years, while Elizabeth's prisoner, Mary plotted against the English queen. Finally losing patience, Elizabeth had her tried in September, 1586, and, despite a bold, brilliant defense of herself, Mary was convicted and beheaded. She died Feb. 8, 1587, calmly reiterating her innocence and chanting in Latin a Catholic prayer to drown out the Protestant minister's English one.

Painter, Poet, Sculptor,
Architect and Engineer

MICHELANGELO

A MASTERPIECE of painting on the ceiling of the Sistine Chapel in Rome owes its existence to political intrigue. Pope Julius II commissioned Michelangelo in 1503 to design and execute the statuary for his tomb, but, influenced by Bramante and quarreling with the great artist, ordered him to paint the ceiling instead. Michelangelo said he was a sculptor rather than a painter and urged Raphael for the task, but had to submit and worked on the magnificent design for four years (1508-1512). Finishing it, he was allowed to return to the more congenial task of the tomb, but Pope Julius died in 1513 and the work was put off. The wonderful statue of Moses is a fragment of this project, which Michelangelo hoped for forty years to complete, but was always disappointed.

Other celebrated sculptures of the master are the marble *Cupid* executed at Florence in 1795 that won him the summons to Rome, the noble *David* carved out of an enormous block of marble, the *Manchester Madonna* in the English National Gallery, a bronze of Pope Julius II, an athletic nude called *Christ Risen,* and the great monument to Giuliano and Lorenzo de Medici. Also the bas-reliefs, *Battle of the Centaurs* and *Madonna of the Steps.*

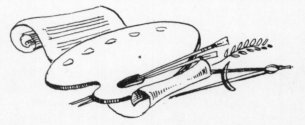

Among his paintings are the celebrated *Last Judgment* in the Sistine Chapel, the circular *Holy Family* in the Uffizi Gallery, the frescoes *Conversion of Paul* and *Martyrdom of Peter* in the Vatican, and the *Battle of Cascina,* done in competition with Leonardo da Vinci for a historical fresco in the Florentine Palazzo Vecchio.

As an architect he planned the completion of St. Peter's Cathedral in Rome and did the Farnese Palace in the same city. He also designed the Medici sepulchral chapel and the Laurentian Library in Florence. And for both cities, in his capacity as military engineer, he designed new fortifications. Michelangelo's poetry was mainly lyric and romantic, but also touched on philosophical and religious subjects.

Born March 6, 1475, at Florence, of a family named Buonarroti, Michelangelo died in Rome, Feb. 18, 1564, one of the most brilliant figures of the Italian Renaissance.

Greatest of
American Humorists

MARK TWAIN
(SAMUEL L. CLEMENS)

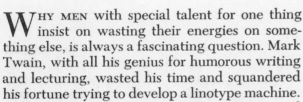

WHY MEN with special talent for one thing insist on wasting their energies on something else, is always a fascinating question. Mark Twain, with all his genius for humorous writing and lecturing, wasted his time and squandered his fortune trying to develop a linotype machine.

The celebrated author of *Tom Sawyer* and *Huckleberry Finn* was born Samuel Langhorne Clemens at Florida, Mo., Nov. 30, 1835, and spent his boyhood at Hannibal, Mo., where he learned the printing trade. As a journeyman printer he worked in St. Louis, New York and Philadelphia, but dropped the trade to become a pilot on the Mississippi. At the time of the Civil War he went West with his brother, prospected for gold in Nevada, made a trip to the Sandwich Islands, and then began writing for the Virginia City *Enterprise* under the name of Mark Twain, an expression used by Mississippi pilots in taking soundings. The first story to bring him fame was *The Jumping Frog of Calaveras County*.

His first full-length book, *Innocents Abroad*, was the result of a trip to the Mediterranean and the Orient for a San Francisco paper. It had great success on both sides of the Atlantic and was rapidly followed by *Roughing It, The Gilded Age* (a collaboration with Charles Dudley Warner), *Tom Sawyer, A Tramp Abroad* (the result of a second trip to Europe), *The Prince and the Pauper* and *Huckleberry Finn*.

Having settled in the East and married Olivia L. Langdon, Mark Twain in 1884 became chief stockholder in a publishing house. Although he obtained for it publication rights to General Grant's immensely profitable memoirs, the business eventually failed. To pay off its debts and make up his own losses in the unworkable linotype venture he was forced to make a lecture trip around the world in the Nineties. This, despite continued success with such new books as *A Connecticut Yankee in King Arthur's Court* (1889), *The American Claimant* (1892) and *Pudd'nhead Wilson* (1894).

Although most of Mark Twain's humor was plain fun, he often used it to point up political corruption and other failures of society. He also wrote and spoke seriously on public questions. He died at Reading, Conn., April 2, 1910.

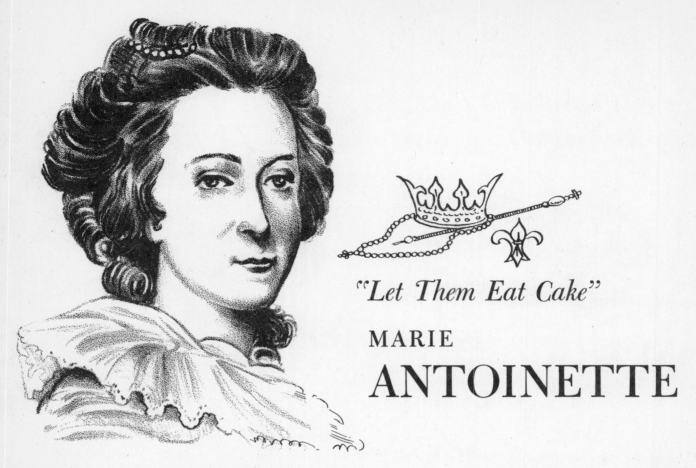

"Let Them Eat Cake"

MARIE ANTOINETTE

Despite the outrageous follies which led directly to her downfall, no one can think of this little Austrian Queen of France without a feeling of compassion, for whatever she lacked in common sense she made up in courage when tragedy finally overtook her.

Daughter of the brilliant Austrian Empress Maria Theresa, Marie was born at Vienna, Nov. 2, 1755, and married at the age of fifteen to the weak-willed and apathetic Duc de Berri, who four years later became Louis XVI of France. It was an unhappy marriage and—even worse in a royal union— for a long while a childless one.

After an enthusiastic coronation Marie quickly and thoroughly antagonized the French people. First she meddled in politics, then shocked conventionalists with her disregard of cumbersome court etiquette, and finally she scandalized everyone by her gaiety and extravagance. Worst of all, she made no secret of her preference for Austria over France.

Events were leading inevitably to the French Revolution. One of the country's chief troubles

was financial, though the peasants groaned under a severe burden of taxation. In such a situation Marie's ostentatious entertainments at Trianon could only make her enemies. At the states-general convoked by Louis May 5, 1789, to consider France's financial disorganization, the assembled delegates blamed Marie and her extravagance for the whole economic débacle.

That fall an attempt at assassination brought home her peril. After months of argument by the King, the royal pair tried to flee the country, but were caught at Varennes and thrown into jail in the Tuileries. A year and a half later Louis was tried and convicted on a charge of conspiring with foreign powers—a charge of which Marie was demonstrably guilty. Louis was guillotined and his widow, after many months of bravely facing indignities, on Oct. 16, 1793, suffered the same fate.

Whether or not she naïvely said, "Let them eat cake," when informed that French peasants lacked bread, the remark was in character.

*The German Composer
Whom England Loved*

MENDELSSOHN

SOMETHING about the spirit of England must have attracted Mendelssohn. His overture to Shakespeare's *Midsummer's Night's Dream* and later his music for the whole play are regarded as best or near-best of his works. And England certainly was attracted to Mendelssohn. Of all the enthusiastic audiences this eminent German composer ever had, two at the Birmingham Festival, held nine years apart (1837 and 1846), were by far the most vociferous. At these he presented his oratorios of *St. Paul* and *Elijah*.

Mendelssohn (Jakob Ludwig Mendelssohn-Bartholdy), born Feb. 3, 1809, at Hamburg, was the Christian grandson of a militant Jewish philosopher, Moses Mendelssohn, who, during the 18th Century, did much to reduce discriminatory legislation against Jews in Germany. The composer's father was converted to Christianity and thereby left his son advantages of education and opportunity in striking contrast with those of the grandfather. The son seized these advantages with surprising zeal.

When talent for music showed itself early, his parents gave him the best instruction available, and Mendelssohn profited by it well enough to appear almost the prodigy that Mozart was. He gave his first public piano concert at the age of nine, in Berlin. The next year he appeared successfully in Paris. In 1824 he began to publish compositions for the piano, violin and violincello.

After concert-traveling through England and the Continent, he became director (1835) of the Leipzig Concerts and in that city, then the musical center of the world, won an outstanding reputation. Besides the *St. Paul* and *Elijah* oratorios, presented in England, his work thereafter included music for Goethe's *Walpurgisnacht,* the *Antigone* and *Oedipus* of Sophocles and many trios, concertos and sonatas. Meeting Jenny Lind in 1844, he composed special music for the famous "Swedish Nightingale."

Mendelssohn's letters, which were translated into English and published in London (1862), revealed him, as his friends knew him, as a man of great charm and noble character. He died at Leipzig, Nov. 4, 1847.

Prophet of the Sword

MOHAMMED

FOUNDER of one of the world's most powerful religions, with many millions of followers in Asia and Africa, Mohammed was forty before he experienced the revelation that led to Islam.

Born at Mecca of poor parents about the year 570, he had little education, though he could probably read and write, despite the Koran's contrary intimation. After working as a sheepherder, he married in his twenty-fifth year a rich widow older than himself and became a partner in a shop selling farm produce.

Christianity and Judaism had already begun to supplant the old pagan religion of Arabia and Mohammed was accustomed to go each year to pray at Mt. Hira, near Mecca. In his fortieth year, during these prayers, the Angel Gabriel appeared, declared him the prophet of God and told him to preach the true religion.

Working slowly at first, Mohammed had only forty followers after four years of preaching. Then he produced some verses telling of the unity of God and the possibility of attaining mercy through prayer, fasting and almsgiving. They were the beginning of the Koran and also the start of wider proselytizing, which as it won him more and more adherents brought down the wrath of other Meccans, who feared for the sacredness of their city. Finally, in the year 622, with 150 followers, he made the journey known as the Hegira to Medina, there becoming a powerful ruler and lawgiver.

Under Jewish influence Mohammed banned certain foods, and later wine, gambling and usury. The warlike nature of his creed stemmed from the caravan-raiding by which his people lived. As his exploits in this direction grew famous, more and more followers trooped to his banner and swore allegiance to Islam.

Warring with the Meccans, Mohammed had indifferent success till 630, when he marched against the city with 10,000 men and it surrendered, recognizing him as chief prophet. Most of the rest of Arabia then honored him as a prince and God's prophet. He was preparing an expedition against Syria when he died on the 8th of June, 632. Just previously he made his last pigrimage to Mecca, drawing up ceremonies for all future pilgrimages.

He Led His People to the Promised Land

MOSES

As a matter of history, there can be no doubt that Moses founded the religion and established the nationality of the Jewish people.

The Bible tells that he was born in Egypt of Levite parents and, when the Pharaoh ordered all new-born male Hebrews to be killed, the infant Moses was placed in an ark of bulrushes and set adrift on the Nile. Found by the Pharaoh's daughter and nursed surreptitiously by his own mother, Moses grew up in the splendor of the court, only to be forced to flee for his life when he killed an Egyptian oppressing a Jew.

In the desert bordering the Red Sea he dwelled quietly for forty years as a shepherd. Then in the episode of the burning bush, God revealed that he was to be the savior of his people. Returning to Egypt, he began with the help of his brother Aaron the appointed task of leading the Children of Israel out of bondage. The Jews were reluctant, however, and the Pharaoh definitely opposed their departure from Egypt. It took the seven plagues, to win the former and badger the latter into assent.

Even then, after Moses had led his followers away, the Egyptian monarch changed his mind another time and took an army in pursuit. Then occurred the miraculous episode of the parting of the waters of the Red Sea, by which the Children of Israel were saved and the hosts of the Pharaoh were destroyed. Convinced now that their leader was chosen of God, the people followed him on the march to Sinai.

But on the long journey to the Promised Land disaffection grew among the various Jewish tribes, and Moses, to placate them, performed miracles proving that God was still with them. Finally, to establish his complete authority, he brought the Ten Commandments down from Mt. Sinai and announced God's covenant with Israel. As the migration approached the River Jordan, scouts were sent forth to explore Canaan. Their report was favorable, but the people were afraid, and for their rebellion they were punished by being compelled to wander in the wilderness until that generation had passed away.

Old and weary, but content that his people's exile would teach them the hard lesson that they needed to learn, Moses toiled up the slopes of Mt. Pisgah to a spot overlooking the valley of the Jordan. There he died alone.

Independence

for All the Americas

JAMES
MONROE

ALTHOUGH Monroe was involved in such momentous affairs as the Louisiana Purchase and the early negotiations to acquire Florida, he is remembered chiefly for the celebrated "Monroe Doctrine," which defined as an act of hostility to the United States any attempt by a foreign power to make further conquests or colonizations on either American continent. No legislation was passed to implement the Doctrine, but it has served as an effective check on many European ambitions.

A close friend of both Jefferson and Madison, Monroe was born in Westmoreland County, Va., Apr. 28, 1758. He left William and Mary College during the Revolution and fought in a number of battles, being wounded at Trenton. After the war he studied law under Jefferson and entered politics, first as a member (1782) of the Virginia legislature. In 1790 he was elected to the U. S. Senate, leaving in 1794 to become Minister to France.

There was a controversy over his purportedly excessive sympathy for the French and he retired to private law practice. In 1799 he became governor of Virginia. In 1803 President Jefferson sent him abroad again in connection with the Louisiana and Florida negotiations, and in 1811 he became Madison's Secretary of State. Five years later, by a huge vote, he won the first of two terms as President.

Under his administration there were few exciting events, but the country prospered greatly and frontiers moved farther westward as five new States were admitted to the Union.

Long public service had made chaos out of his private affairs and after retiring to his Virginia estate from the White House he had to ask Congress for reimbursement of his European expenses. In 1826 he was awarded $30,000. He died during a visit to New York, July 4, 1831.

Lacking the brilliance of some of his great contemporaries, Monroe nevertheless had, in the words of John Quincy Adams, "a mind . . . sound in its ultimate judgments, and firm in its final conclusions." His famous Doctrine has been successfully invoked on a number of occasions, against Spain, France and Great Britain.

Child Prodigy

Who Grew Up

to be a Genius

WOLFGANG AMADEUS
MOZART

OFTEN too young a display of talent burns its owner out, but the composer Mozart began his musical career at the incredible age of three and went on to become one of the 18th Century's greatest artists.

Born Jan. 27, 1756, at Salzburg, Austria, the son of a fine violinist, Mozart breathed music almost as soon as he breathed air. At the age of four he was accomplished on the clavichord and had composed a number of minuets. At six he went with his sister (almost as talented as he) and his father to Munich and Vienna and so impressed Emperor Francis I and the Elector of Bavaria that they were delighted to offer patronage. The following year the Mozart youngsters astounded music circles in Paris and London. At ten Mozart was composing symphonies that were produced and sonatas that were published. At twelve he wrote and conducted the music for the dedication of the Orphan House Church in Vienna. At thirteen he was made director of concerts given by the Archbishop of Salzburg. At fourteen he had his opera *Mithridates* performed in Milan.

About 1779 he was appointed composer to the imperial court at Vienna. He fell in love with a singer named Aloysia Weber and his opera,

Idomeneo (1780), is supposed to have been written to win her favor. If so, it failed, and two years later he married a younger sister, Constance Weber. Her extravagance compounded his financial difficulties, already formidable, since the imperial appointment offered more dignity than money, and Mozart had to waste his limited strength in concert tours and teaching. After production of his operas, *The Marriage of Figaro* and *Don Giovanni*, and a generous offer from the king of Prussia, his imperial patrons were reminded to give him some relief, but by then it was a little late.

During his work on *The Magic Flute* (produced in 1791), the story goes, a mysterious stranger called on Mozart and asked him, in secrecy, to write a requiem mass, promising to call for it later, The composer, ill and fast losing strength, felt that he was writing his own requiem. On Dec. 5, 1791, a part of the mass was ready to rehearse, but Mozart was too exhausted to participate with the friends who came to help him. At midnight of the same day he died.

The Singing Emperor

NERO

MURDER, profligacy and extravagance were the distinguishing marks of Nero's regime. Among the individuals he killed were his mother, two wives, the son of his benefactor, the poet Lucan and a woman who refused to marry him. On the wholesale scale, Christians were the chief victims of his blood lust, many dying in agony under torture when he blamed them for the burning of Rome (64 A.D.). Ancient report has it that Nero himself started the fire, simply for the sake of a spectacle, and sang and played the harp while two-thirds of the great city was consumed.

It was adoption by Emperor Claudius that brought Nero to the throne as sixth Roman Emperor. Born at Antinum Dec. 15, 37 A.D., of Agrippina and Domitius Ahenobarbus, he came to power in 54 when his mother, whose second marriage was with Claudius, had the Emperor poisoned. Despite his outrageous cruelties later, Nero seems to have made a promising start as head of the government and much of the responsibility for his subsequent misbehavior is

laid to Agrippina's evil influence. She paid the penalty in 59, being killed to please Nero's mistress Poppaea Sabina, who also persuaded him to murder his wife and marry her. Later Nero kicked Poppaea to death.

After the burning of Rome, Nero began its rebuilding on a far more magnificent scale, with an especially splendid palace for himself on the Palatine Hill. To pay the enormous expense of this work he plundered the rest of the Empire, making enemies who eventually contrived his downfall. One such plot failed in 65, when Nero discovered the ringleaders and put them to death. Along with Lucan, the poet, Piso, Faenius Rufus, Seneca and many others lost their lives.

In 68, however, Roman legions in France and Spain revolted and the Praetorian Guards at home took advantage of the situation to make Galba Emperor. Nero fled and as his pursuers approached, June 11, he committed suicide.

As vain as he was cruel, Nero had tried unsuccessfully to make a reputation as a poet, philosopher, musician, actor and charioteer.

"Man of Destiny"

NAPOLEON
BONAPARTE

THE list of the Corsican-born French Emperor's military victories is long and brilliant, but his best-remembered battle was his final defeat at Waterloo. The troops he led loved, trusted and followed him unquestioningly, but Europe refused to be dominated by a despot and, though it took half a dozen coalitions of the Powers to do it, his downfall was inevitable.

Born Aug. 15, 1769, he went to military schools in Paris and Brienne, and had his first taste of success at the siege of Toulon (1793), where his characteristic concentration of artillery decided the day. Successful campaigns in Italy rapidly followed and by 1797 Napoleon was a national hero. That year he was given command of an expedition against Egypt, which had as its ultimate goal the conquest of India. Victorious in land battles, he lost his fleet to Nelson at the Nile and the grandiose project, cut off from home bases, gradually dwindled away, Napoleon returning to Paris in the fall of 1799. There he overturned the Government and had himself made first consul.

His talent as an administrator and law-giver, almost equal to his military genius, now came into play. Quickly restoring order to the disorganized government, he went on to stabilize finances, improve the courts, encourage education and supervise a brilliantly systematic codification of French laws.

Made Emperor May 18, 1804, he divorced his first wife, Josephine, who had provided no heirs, and in 1810 married Marie Louise, daughter of the Austrian Emperor. Two years later came the disastrous Russian adventure, on which he won battles, as always, but lost almost his whole army in the desperate winter retreat from Moscow. In 1813 Prussia and Austria joined Russia to defeat him at Leipzig and he was forced to abdicate the first time, April 11, 1814.

Escaping from imprisonment at Elba, Napoleon had another brief moment of triumph, only to be crushed by Blucher and Wellington at Waterloo, June 18, 1815. His exile to St. Helena ended with his death, May 5, 1821.

[115]

Why Did the Apple Fall?

SIR ISAAC
NEWTON

Newton's own momentous discoveries in science, including the law of gravitation, differential calculus and valuable theories of light and color, were almost equalled in importance by the work other men did under his encouragement.

It is Voltaire's story that Newton began pondering the question of gravitation when he saw an apple fall in his garden. He was twenty-three at the time, having been born Dec. 25, 1642, at Woolsthorpe, England, and educated at Cambridge, where he received a thorough grounding in mathematics. Other scientists had been aware that some such force as gravity pulled objects toward the earth and was exerted between celestial bodies. But not till Newton's lengthy researches were the exact laws of that force established—that it varied directly with the product of any two masses and inversely with the square of the distance between them.

His experiments with light and color, which, among other things, led to his devising a reflect-

ing telescope, brought him such prestige in scientific circles that he was elected to membership in the Royal Society at the astonishingly early age of twenty-nine. He became its president in 1703 and was reelected to the office each year till he died on March 27, 1727. The position enabled him to give especially useful aid to other scientists and inventors, like John Falmsteed, the astronomer of whose book, *Greenwich Observations*, he supervised the publication, and John Harrison, whom he helped to devise and perfect the chronometer.

When King James II began meddling with English universities, Newton went actively into politics on the side of learning, serving in Parliament. This political activity resulted, in 1696, in his appointment first as warden then master of the mint, an office he held the rest of his life.

Leibnitz, the German scientist, arrived at a system of differential calculus independently of Newton and the question of which made the discovery first has caused bitter argument. Modern opinion gives Newton credit in point of time, but Leibnitz praise for better methods. Newton is buried in Westminster Abbey.

From Anglican Minister to Catholic Cardinal

HENRY CARDINAL
NEWMAN

OF MODERN Englishmen desiring to repair the historic schism with Rome, which under Henry VIII laid the foundation for the Church of England, Cardinal Newman was the most famous and influential. A preacher and writer of great power, he led back to the Roman Catholic Church not only laymen, but hundreds of Anglican ministers as well.

Born at London, Feb. 21, 1801, the son of a banker, Newman at fifteen was "converted" to religion, a vivid experience of which all his life he said he was "more certain than that he had hands or feet." Three years after his graduation (1821) from Oxford he became an Anglican minister, working at the university. A religious difference with the provost brought his resignation in 1832 and a trip through the Mediterranean on which he wrote *Lead, Kindly Light.*

On his return to Oxford in 1833 he became interested in the Oxford Movement, a group of High Church clergymen dedicated to fight for "the apostolical succession and the integrity of the Prayer-Book." During the next eight years Newman's sermons and *Tracts of the Times,* ninety of which were published, had great influence in determining doctrine and ritual within the Movement. But in 1841 he began to doubt his own theological position. Retiring to seclusion with a small band of followers, he lived a

monastic life until, in 1843, he published as an anonymous advertisement in the *Oxford Conservative Journal* a retraction of everything he had said against the Catholic Church. That same year he resigned from his ministry, but it was not until 1845 that he was received into the Catholic Church. The following year, at Rome, he was ordained a priest.

Back in England he lived most of his last forty years in seclusion. But there were interruptions. In a London sermon he charged an anti-Catholic ex-Dominican friar of immorality and was sued for libel, losing a hundred-pound verdict. His own large legal expenses (£14,000) were paid by enthusiastic public subscription.

Beginning in 1864, he published his religious autobiography *(Apologia pro vita sua),* a work of extraordinary interest, to vindicate himself with the mass of educated Englishmen, who had been dubious about his career since 1841.

It was in 1879 that Pope Leo XIII made him Cardinal—an unusual honor for a simple English priest and one which brought applause from the whole English-speaking world. Cardinal Newman died Aug. 11, 1890, at Edgbaston.

"The Lady with the Lamp"

FLORENCE NIGHTINGALE

BOTH nurses and patients of modern hospitals owe an inestimable debt of gratitude to this heroic English gentlewoman. No single individual did more to make nursing the sanitary, scientific procedure that it is today.

After a childhood spent mostly in England—though she was born May 12, 1820, in the Italian city for which she was named—Florence Nightingale heeded her philanthropic mother's advice and refused to content herself with a conventional socal life. Hospital work interested her and she was able to make an exhaustive study of institutions in London, Edinburgh, and on the Continent, as well as to take nurse's training courses in Paris and at Kaiserswerth on the Rhine. By 1858 she had earned enough reputation to be made superintendent of the Hospital for Invalid Gentlewomen in London.

It was the Crimean War, however, that brought her world fame. Early in that conflict the English people were angered at reports of bad care for wounded soldiers. Miss Nightingale offered her services to the secretary of war, Sidney Herbert, who was a childhood friend, and went (November, 1854) with thirty-eight other nurses to the Crimea. Her job was to supervise army hospitals and run the entire nursing staff, caring for 10,000 sick and wounded men.

Working like a Hercules, often as long as twenty hours a day, she cleaned up hospitals and barracks, made personal rounds of the patients and spent all the time she could spare in operating rooms, comforting and encouraging the shattered men. Between February and June, 1855, her indefatigable efforts reduced the death rate from forty-two per cent to two per cent. Although seriously ill of Crimean fever, she refused to leave her post till the British evacuated Turkey in July, 1856. By this time her glorious work was so widely appreciated that the British Government sent a man-of-war to take her home.

She used a 50,000-pound fund raised in recognition of her service to start the Nightingale Nurses' Training Home at St. Thomas's Hospital, and at her urging modern nursing schools were set up elsewhere. Her advice on military hospital care was sought later during the Civil War in America, the Indian Mutiny and the Franco-Prussian War. She lived to be ninety, dying at London, Aug. 13, 1910.

*America's
Outstanding
Playwright*

EUGENE GLADSTONE
O'NEILL

No other American dramatist approaches the stature of this quiet ex-seaman. Even his less successful plays, such as *The Iceman Cometh* (1946), rouse more interest than any other contemporary writer's.

Eugene Gladstone O'Neill was born at New York City, Oct. 16, 1888, the son of a well-known actor, James O'Neill. After attending Catholic schools, he went briefly to Princeton (1906-1907), then spent the two years at sea as a merchant sailor from which he derived so much material for his plays. Returning to land, he wandered about the United States and Central and South America in a variety of businesses, even performing at one time as a vaudeville actor in a cut-down version of his father's successful production, *Monte Christo.*

Hospitalization for suspected tuberculosis brought reflection on his varied experiences and he began his dramatic writing. The summer of 1916 found him on Cape Cod as one of the "Provincetown group" of writers and actors who operated a resort theatre in hot weather and presented their plays at the Provincetown Theatre in New York during the winters. O'Neill's first

full-length play, *Beyond the Horizon,* was published in 1920, and won the Pulitzer Prize. Next in 1921, came *Emperor Jones,* the powerful story of a Negro railroad porter who became emperor of a tropical island. In 1922 he won another Pulitzer Prize with *Anna Christie,* and had two other plays produced, in one of which, *The Hairy Ape,* he first used masks to show the difference between characters as they are and as they seem to others.

He had many other successes during the 1920's, including the controversial *Desire Under the Elms* (1924), *The Great God Brown* (1926), *Lazarus Laughed* and *Dynamo* (1929). It was *Strange Interlude,* however, that established him on the top rung of the theatrical ladder—a five-hour-long drama notable for reviving the ancient device of the "aside." It won O'Neill's third Pulitzer Prize. Another five-hour drama, *Mourning Becomes Electra,* appeared in 1931 and three years later the comedy *Ah Wilderness,* in which George M. Cohan made a personal triumph. After years of silence O'Neill unveiled *The Iceman Cometh* in 1946. It missed the critical acclaim of many previous works.

Founder of the City of Brotherly Love

WILLIAM

PENN

ALTHOUGH he bore arms in Ireland and earlier in the Dutch War, William Penn was a "fighting" Quaker only in the true sense of life-long devotion to and peaceful activity in defense of tolerance and the individual's right to choose his own religion.

A Londoner and son of a prominent British admiral, he was born Oct. 14, 1644, and attached himself zealously to the Quaker faith while at Oxford. His expulsion from college was the first of many troubles his profound belief engendered, for imprisonment as a Quaker occurred to him repeatedly. After traveling on the Continent and going on business to Ireland for his father (here came the military part of his career), he began preaching and writing against orthodox Christian beliefs. During a resultant term in London Tower (1668) he wrote two of his most popular books, *No Cross, No Crown* and *Innocency with her Open Face*.

Long interested in America, Penn in 1681 obtained the territorial charter named for his father in lieu of a debt owed by the English government. The next year he led a group of persecuted fellow-religionists to the site of present-day Philadelphia and, immediately making friends with the Indians, set up a tolerant colony that attracted settlers from everywhere. He stayed two years in Philadelphia, establishing a liberal constitution and using his own authority with wisdom, then returned to Europe.

With James II Penn had considerable influence and won important concessions, including release of 1,200 imprisoned Quakers. But under William III things went less smoothly, Penn several times being accused of treason, though never seriously enough to endanger his life. In 1699 he returned to Pennsylvania when a variety of troubles threatened the colony. Another two-year stay resulted in the repression of piracy, which had flourished on the Friends' reluctance to use arms, and a profitable treaty with the Indians.

In his last years Penn had money troubles, partly caused by his dishonest agent in America, and he suffered from epileptic fits. He died at Ruscombe in Berkshire, England, July 30, 1718.

[120]

Magician
with Microbes

LOUIS
PASTEUR

THIS quiet, hard-working French chemist and physicist did his most dramatic work in discovering a remedy for the dreadful disease of rabies. Thousands of human lives have been saved by his patient experimentation and the cry of "Mad dog!" no longer has the power to terrify that it had before his time.

The son of a tanner, Louis Pasteur was born at Dôle, Dec. 27, 1822, and graduated from the Ecole Normale, Paris, in 1847. He first taught as professor of physics at Dijon, then shifted to chemistry at Strassburg, where his chief interest was the "diseases" of beer and wine, long a puzzle to chemists. The exact process of fermentation, its causes and effects were not known, and Pasteur applied himself tirelessly to discover them. Undeterred by the discouragement of friends, he worked till he was sure that minute organisms were the cause. In 1872 he published his famous essay on fermentation, and beer and wine making promptly changed from a haphazard to a scientific activity.

Before this, in 1865, the silk industry of southern France was endangered by a disease attacking silkworms. Pasteur's friend, Dumas, pleaded with him to do something and, though he had never before seen a silkworm, within a few months he discovered the bacilli causing two variations of the disease and suggested curatives that saved the industry. The practical control of anthrax, a devastating animal disease, is also owing to Pasteur, who devised a weakened culture of the bacilli with which to inoculate cattle. Chicken cholera he treated similarly.

Pasteur not only had the enormous patience to develop and experiment with his rabies treatment on dogs, but also the courage to try it for the first time on a human being, in 1885. Three years later the Pasteur Institute was founded in Paris and as a result of the spread of such institutions over the world the death rate from hydrophobia is now less than one per cent.

A simple, affectionate, noble man, who believed in hard work and cared nothing for profit, Pasteur lived a happy life with his devoted wife and died at St. Cloud, Sept. 28, 1895.

His Tales of the East Enchanted Europe

MARCO
POLO

Probably the most celebrated traveler of all time, Marco Polo was born in the year 1254 at Venice, of a noble family. His father and uncle, in the manner of Venetians of the time, were abroad at the time of his birth, visiting the great Kublai Khan, later Mongol emperor of all China. Returning to Italy in 1269, the elder Polos, on order from Kublai, tried to recruit a hundred European artists and scientists to take back to China, but, failing, took young Marco.

They crossed the Gobi Desert and arrived at Kublai's Shangtui court in 1275. The young traveler almost immediately won the Mongol emperor's fancy, and was sent as emissary to such distant places as Burma, Cochin China and southern India. Kublai even made him governor of one of his provinces later.

After a long stay in China, the Polos won the Emperor's reluctant permission to go home and sailed with a Mongol princess by way of Sumatra and southern India to Persia, thence arriving finally in Venice in 1295, twenty-four years after their departure. Although they returned with a fortune in jewels and silks, they were at first denied recognition and even refused entrance to their own mansion.

In 1298 Marco Polo subscribed a galley for Venice in the war with the Genoese and on it, in the battle of Curzola Island, Sept. 7, he was taken prisoner. He spent a year in jail in Genoa and it was here that he began writing the story of his travels, dictating to a fellow prisoner. In July or August of 1299 he was released and little else is known of his life, except that on Jan. 9, 1324, he called a priest and a notary to make his will, and died the same day.

Marco Polo's narrative of his travels described the history and customs of various Eastern countries, concentrating on Jenghiz Khan and his grandson, Kublai. For a long time it was almost the only European source of information on the Orient. Many of his stories were so colorful that he was suspected of fictionalizing, but modern research has verified their essential accuracy.

"Lafayette, We Are Here"

JOHN J.
PERSHING

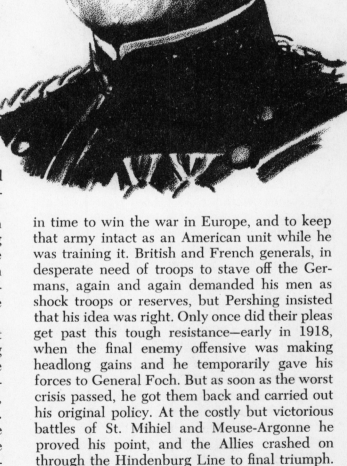

"B LACK JACK" learned his toughness the hard way, in campaigns against the Apache Indians (1886) in Arizona and the Sioux (1890) in the Dakotas; at Santiago during the Cuban War; in the Philippines, where by combining diplomacy with force he subdued the savage Moros in 1903; and on the Mexican border in 1916, when he chased the wily bandit, Francisco Villa. By the time his greatest task came along, in 1917, he was ready.

Born Sept. 13, 1860, at Laclede, Mo., he got an appointment to West Point after attending normal school. Following his Indian service he taught military science at the University of Nebraska, at the same time winning a law degree, then returned to West Point as an instructor. In 1906, after his successful dealing with the Moros in the Philippines, President Theodore Roosevelt promoted him from captain to brigadier-general over the heads of 862 senior officers.

When war was declared with Germany in 1917, President Wilson made Pershing commander of American troops. He had two chief problems: to build a trained army from nothing in time to win the war in Europe, and to keep that army intact as an American unit while he was training it. British and French generals, in desperate need of troops to stave off the Germans, again and again demanded his men as shock troops or reserves, but Pershing insisted that his idea was right. Only once did their pleas get past this tough resistance—early in 1918, when the final enemy offensive was making headlong gains and he temporarily gave his forces to General Foch. But as soon as the worst crisis passed, he got them back and carried out his original policy. At the costly but victorious battles of St. Mihiel and Meuse-Argonne he proved his point, and the Allies crashed on through the Hindenburg Line to final triumph.

After the war Pershing was honored with a permanent rank of full general, previously held only by Washington, Grant, Sherman and Sheridan. He became Chief of Staff in 1921, retired in 1924, and died July 15, 1948.

Short Story Master

WILLIAM SIDNEY
PORTER
(O. HENRY)

No other writer has had such influence as O. Henry on the modern American popular short story. He developed the "twist," or surprise ending, to such perfection that he is given credit for inventing it. The aim of most big-circulation magazines, and their fiction writers, still is to equal his dexterity with "snappers." But his talent went deeper than this. It involved great skill in all the phases of story-telling. It also involved a love of the romantic, the picturesque and the oddities in life—and a genius for reporting them that gave his work lasting value

O. Henry's own life was a combination of success and tragedy. Born William Sydney Porter, Sept. 11, 1862, at Greensboro, N. C., he left school at the age of fifteen to clerk in his uncle's drug store. At twenty, he went West for his health, spending two years on a Texas ranch. Afterwards he wandered through the South, the Southwest and Central America.

In 1896 he was accused of embezzling from an Austin, Tex., bank where he had worked five years earlier. The true circumstances have never been clearly established, but he was convicted and sent to prison, an experience of special horror to anyone as sensitive and reserved as O. Henry. His first story acceptances from important magazines came while he was awaiting trial, and during his thirty-nine months' imprisonment he did a great deal of writing.

In 1902 he moved to New York City, which he named "Bagdad on the Subway" and grew to love and understand far better than most of its inhabitants. Penetrating its out-of-the-way corners, he talked to derelicts and workers in strange occupations, and ended with the wealth of curious information that made his stories so fascinating.

Contributing regularly to the New York *World,* and various magazines, O. Henry soon had material for the short story collections (*The Four Million, The Voice of the City, The Gift of the Wise Men,* etc.) that toward the end of his life brought him wealth and fame.

He died June 5, 1910, in New York City.

Father of Cubism

PABLO
PICASSO

IN modern art there is no more influential name than Picasso. For the school of Cubists, Cézanne sometimes has been called the initiator, but most critics feel his love of nature would have made him disown the experimenters.

Picasso, though he trained his genius in France and is thoroughly identified with French art, was born at Málaga, Spain, Oct. 2, 1881, the son of an artist who taught at the Academy of Barcelona. Under him Pablo took his first instruction, but after many visits to Paris settled there in 1903.

His early work was relatively conservative, somewhat in the manner of Toulouse-Lautrec, with clear contours, well-planned spacing and the coloring usually a cool greenish-gray. His subjects were from the circus and the seamier side of big city life—acrobats, girls of Montmartre and the like.

Then, in the period roughly from 1906 to 1910, he and George Braque worked out the Cubist formula. Braque was first to make an innovation, putting into his designs real printed paper and nails. Then Picasso added pieces of wood and other things, till they had a form of art that was both painting and sculpture. Their idea was to avoid all imitation of nature's forms, to create an entirely abstract language of form with which to convey profound reality. "For reality alone," said Picasso, "even when concealed, has power to arouse emotion."

He returned to natural form after 1918, with wonderfully clear and economically executed outlines, and increased his stature as a painter. But his inventiveness continued and inspired many followers. Negro sculpture, with its strange expressiveness, impressed him early. He was interested in the stage, too, and designed scenery, curtains and costumes for Russian ballets, and collaborated with Jean Cocteau (1917) in the ballet *Parade*, creating others by himself later. He also drew portraits of artists and writers, illustrated books and did etchings.

His most recent innovation, going back some years, is called the "simultaneous view" or "circulating viewpoint," by which he shows faces full-front and in profile of the same figure, to give a more comprehensive feel of character. These have been mostly faces of women.

PLATO

Although Plato is generally considered the greatest philosophical writer of all times, the fact that he wrote dialogues quoting real people, but never himself, has made it a long-debated question how much of the philosophy was his own and how much that of Socrates and the other thinkers he named.

Originally called Aristocles, Plato was born about 427 B.C., probably in Athens, and had the usual education of youths of good family, studying literature, music and mathematics. He wrote poetry and made a name for himself as an athlete. At the age of twenty he began an eight-year period of study under Socrates, but never, apparently, was on as intimate a footing with the elder philosopher as some of his other disciples: he was not present, for example, at the famous conversation of friends preceding Socrates's suicide.

After the death of his master, Plato seems to have traveled widely, to Cyrene, Egypt, Italy and Sicily, also to have studied with Euclid at Megara. About 388 B.C., he was captured and sold into slavery, later being ransomed by friends. Back finally in Athens, he established the celebrated Academy, which he considered his life work and where he taught for the last forty years of his career, chiefly by the discussion method derived from Socrates.

This Academy, in a sense the first university, lasted for 800 years and produced many outstanding men, the most famous of whom was Aristotle. Plato's disciples made particularly great progress in mathematics, but other sciences and the arts were not neglected.

It is curious that, in spite of his absorption in political theory, Plato was so much less active in public affairs than his contemporaries. His one venture, as tutor to the Syracusan king, came late in his life and was a failure.

Most famous of Plato's dialogues is the *Republic*, in which he outlined what to him was the ideal government. Others developed a philosophy in which ideas were emphasized as "the most real existences." The influence of his writings has been tremendous — even greater than that of Aristotle. Plato died at eighty, in 347 B.C., while at a wedding feast in Athens.

A Titan of Painting

REMBRANDT

IRONICALLY reversing the fate of most great painters, Rembrandt Harmens van Rijn at the age of twenty-five leaped to fame as Amsterdam's finest portrait painter, then outlived his popularity and died in the poverty that most young artists have to endure. But subsequent lovers of art have securely established him among history's immortals.

Born July 15, 1606, at Leyden, Holland, the son of a wealthy miller, Rembrandt was intended for a profession, but early made up his own mind as to a career. He studied for something over three years in his native city and Amsterdam, then began painting seriously at Leyden in 1626. Five years later his reputation had grown enough for prominent citizens of Amsterdam to persuade him to move there, where he spent the rest of his life.

The three periods into which his works are divided are rather sharply marked by his use of prevailing colors. Up till 1640 greenish-gray was dominant. His magnificent group portrait, *Lesson in Anatomy*, was of this tone, as were the portraits of Martin Daey and his wife, and the *Danaë*, which so beautifully proved his mastery of the female figure. In his second period golden-brown predominated, and produced such masterpieces as *The Night Watch*, his pictures of the Holy Family, the *Good Samaritan*, and the *Woman Taken in Adultery*. From about 1654 on he used dull reds, grays and yellows, with the final, full power of his art, to achieve *John the Baptist Preaching*, *Syndics of the Cloth Hall*, the *Jewish Bride* and *Family Group*.

The prodigious number of Rembrandt's paintings has been estimated as high as nearly a thousand. But he was also an etcher of equal genius, both as an artist and technician, whose landscapes, portraits and Bible stories are invaluable collectors' items.

In his youth and old age, particularly, Rembrandt liked to paint self-portraits; no less than sixty-two of these have been catalogued. He also painted his mother, wife and mistress.

Declared bankrupt in 1656, he had to sell his whole collection of paintings for a pittance and from then to the end of his life suffered in poverty. He died Oct. 4, 1669.

Not Gold, but Potatoes and Tobacco

SIR WALTER
RALEIGH

A SWASHBUCKLING, legendary figure, favorite of Queen Elizabeth, explorer, soldier, colonizer, writer—Sir Walter Raleigh won permanent fame by discovering tobacco and potatoes.

Born about 1552, the handsome, gallant young man spent a year or two at Oxford before his first appearance in history, as one of a group of English volunteers who fought with the French Huguenots. After some five years in France, he joined his half-brother, Sir Humphrey Gilbert, in an exploring project, for which Sir Humphrey obtained a patent in 1578 —"to explore and seize any foreign territory not the possession of a Christian prince or people." Capture of Spanish galleons seems to have been the real purpose of this venture.

In 1580 Raleigh was twice arrested for dueling and also took part in suppressing the Desmonds' Irish rebellion. It was after this that he met Elizabeth, carrying dispatches to the Court. He promptly made the most of his opportunity, winning favors from the Queen far out of proportion to the value of his services in Ireland. His knighthood came in 1584 and two years later 40,000 acres of confiscated Irish land.

When his half-brother died, Raleigh received the renewal of his exploration patent, and in 1584 he sent an expedition to America, which sailed northward along the coast from Florida. The following year he made the first of three unsuccessful efforts to set up colonies in Virginia. Their main result was the introduction of tobacco and potatoes into England.

Sir Walter's influence with Elizabeth fell off when the Earl of Essex came to power and in 1592 she had him imprisoned in the Tower of London over an intrigue with one of her maids of honor. In 1595 he made an expedition to South America, bringing back the first mahogany seen in England. In 1596 he regained the Queen's favor by gallantry at the capture of Cadiz, but after James I came to the throne his properties were taken from him and he was convicted of conspiracy. Temporarily reprieved, he searched for gold in South America. Failing to find it, he was rearrested after his return and executed Oct. 29, 1618.

He Worked Twenty Years on a Statue

AUGUSTE
RODIN

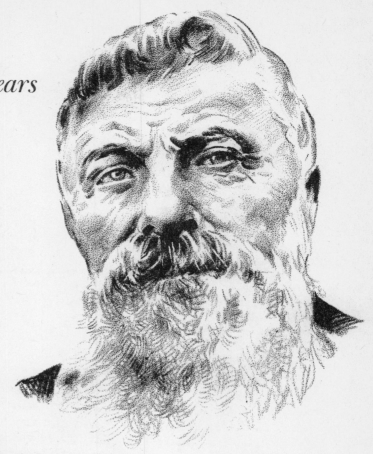

Everyone has seen a picture or copy, at least, of *The Thinker*, and recognized at once the power of the sculptor, Auguste Rodin. Certainly the leader of 19th Century French sculptors, he also belongs among the select company of all-time immortals.

A Parisian, he was born Nov. 10, 1840, and suffered the young artist's traditional poverty. In 1864 he had to give up his only formal training in art, under Barye, for lack of money. Fortunately, a job in the studio of Carrier-Belleuse not only provided a small livelihood, but gave him practice in the mechanical processes of his craft, such as casting. He held it till 1870, when the Germans besieged Paris and he left to serve with the National Guard.

After the Franco-Prussian War he went to Brussels and worked with the Belgian artist, Van Rasbourg, on the statuary of the Bourse, a project that lasted seven years. Meanwhile, his own work went on and began to be exhibited. In 1875 he showed the *Portrait of Garnier* and at the Salon, when he had returned to Paris two years later, *The Bronze Age*. Busts of various artists followed, one of Victor Hugo being exhibited in 1884.

The next year he began his monumental labors on the *Portal of Hell*, a multi-figured representation of Dante's *Inferno*, on which he spent most of the next twenty years. But he also did statues on commission for the towns of Damvillers, Nancy and Calais. And in 1898 he exhibited a beautiful marble work called *The Kiss*, depicting Paolo and Francesca.

In 1899 an incident revealed Rodin's good nature. His sketches for a bust of Balzac had been turned down and the commission given to Falguière. To prove the rejection did not alter his friendship for the other artist, Rodin did a bust of him and showed it at the same exhibition in which Falguière's Balzac was hung.

Rodin succeeded James McNeill Whistler as president of the International Society of Sculptors, Painters and Engravers in 1904. His two most famous statues, *The Thinker* and *The Hand of God*, were done at about this time. But he continued actively producing to the end of his life. He died Nov. 17, 1917.

[129]

The Midnight Rider Who Roused a Nation

PAUL
REVERE

LONGFELLOW made this Boston silversmith famous with his poem, *The Midnight Ride of Paul Revere*. His less fictionalized accomplishments had more importance, though the farmers between Charlestown and Lexington were undoubtedly interested to hear about the British.

He was born New Year's Day of 1735 and had little schooling in his Boston youth, aside from the trade secrets of a gold and silver smith, which he learned from his father. Later he took up copper engraving and printed a number of anti-British caricatures before the Revolution. A thorough-going Tory-hater, he was one of the leaders of the Boston Tea Party.

As official courier of the Massachusetts Provincial Assembly, Revere was sent in December, 1774, to urge the inhabitants of Portsmouth, N. H., to seize British military supplies there. He persuaded them to capture Ft. William and Mary—one of the first military acts of the Revolution. His celebrated midnight ride occurred April 18-19 the following year.

Later in 1775 the Assembly sent him to Philadelphia to learn about the operation of the only powder mill then existing in the colonies. He was allowed only to walk through the building, but his senses and memory were sharp enough to bring back information enabling him to set up a workable factory in Canton. This was worth at least a dozen midnight rides.

In April, 1776, he became a major of infantry in the Massachusetts militia and was promoted to lieutenant-colonel of artillery in November. Later he commanded Castle William, the fort defending Boston harbor. In 1778 he went on a foray to Rhode Island and in 1779 took part in the unsuccessful Penobscot expedition, returning from which he was courtmartialed for disobeying orders, but acquitted.

After the war he manufactured gold and silver ware, and was the first American to produce copper spikes and copper plating for ships. A solid Boston citizen, he was elected Grand Master of the Masons in 1795 and later had the honor of laying the cornerstone of the new State House. He died May 10, 1818.

The Fighting President

THEODORE
ROOSEVELT

THERE are many things to tell about "Teddy" Roosevelt. The paradoxes alone are formidable—a rich man who espoused the common people's cause, a childhood weakling who turned into the hardy "Rough Rider" chieftain, a historian who not only wrote but made history, a naturalist who found his specimens on hair-raising explorations, a Nobel Peace Prize winner who urged war—the list is endless.

Born in New York City Oct. 27, 1858, and educated at Harvard and Columbia Law School, Roosevelt entered politics at the age of twenty-three, as a state assemblyman, and promptly established himself as a fighter against corruption. Two years on a North Dakota ranch interrupted his political career, but he returned to run unsuccessfully for mayor of New York City in 1886. Then he served six years with the U. S. Civil Service Commission and two years as police commissioner of New York, manfully fighting graft in both jobs.

In 1897 he became Assistant Secretary of the Navy and prepared the fleet for the war with Spain that he was sure would ensue. After it was over he returned an Army hero, as a result of the charge up San Juan Hill, and won the governorship of New York. A single term of struggle with political boss Platt got him kicked upstairs, against his will, into the Vice-Presidency. Less than a year later President McKinley was shot and Roosevelt became President.

His seven years in office were notable for the first effective government regulation of "big business," for U. S. acquisition of the Panama Canal Zone, for Roosevelt's diplomatic help in ending the Russo-Japanese War (this won him the Nobel prize), and for his vigorous support of the conservation movement. He declined to run for a third term in 1908, but in 1912 he did run again, splitting the Republican vote and giving the election to Wilson. Afterwards he made celebrated expeditions through Africa and Brazil. When World War I broke out he urged the United States to join the Allies at once and bitterly fought Wilson for his neutrality.

As a writer Roosevelt is best known for his *Naval War of 1812*, and for his articles in *Outlook*. He died Jan. 5, 1919, at Oyster Bay, N. Y.

Fighter for the
Four Freedoms

FRANKLIN DELANO
ROOSEVELT

PERHAPS the most powerful political personality of modern times, F. D. R. left the imprint of his philosophy on the United States—an imprint that will not easily be eradicated.

In many respects his career paralleled that of his distant cousin, Theodore Roosevelt. He was born of wealthy parents, Jan. 30, 1882, at Hyde Park, N. Y., and, like "Teddy," was educated at Harvard and Columbia Law School. Similarly, he began his political climb in the New York State Legislature and served as Assistant Secretary of the Navy. His tenure in the Navy Department (1913-1920) gave him enough national prominence to cause his nomination by the Democrats for the Vice-Presidency in 1920. The Republicans, however, won in a landslide.

In 1921 Roosevelt was crippled by infantile paralysis, but after a long, courageous struggle regained his health and returned to politics, being elected Governor of New York in 1928. Continuing the liberal course of his predecessor, Alfred E. Smith, he pushed reform legislation and, as the Great Depression deepened, became the logical candidate for the Presidency. When

he took office, in March, 1933, the country was in desperate economic condition.

With his magnificent flair for the dramatic, F. D. R. at once banished the fear which he said was all the nation had to fear. In the famous first "Hundred Days" of his Administration he set in furious motion a sweeping program of economic and social reform, intended—like his cousin's before him—to bring American institutions in tune with the times. Much of the "New Deal" seemed radical to conservatives, but it was essentially conservative, designed to preserve the country, and was so accepted by the electorate, who gave F. D. R. an unprecedented series of four terms as President. The Supreme Court invalidated some of the laws and Roosevelt's one major set-back came when he tried to "pack" it, but new appointments finally gave him a sympathetic Court.

His conduct of World War II was characteristically bold, vigorous and successful, but the monumental efforts it took cost him his life before final victory, on April 12, 1945.

Discoverer of X-Rays

WILHELM KONRAD

von ROENTGEN

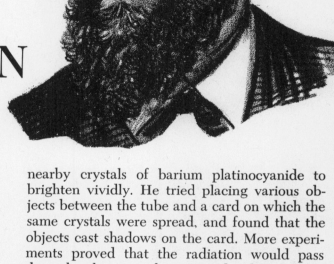

MORE THAN a hundred years before Roentgen, William Morgan is believed to have produced X-rays, but, unlike Roentgen in 1895, he failed to recognize their nature. As a matter of fact, the discovery was largely accidental with Roentgen and he was so uncertain of what he had found that he applied the term X (symbol of unknown) to the rays that later bore his name.

A Prussian, born at Lennep March 27, 1845, Roentgen was educated in Holland and at the University of Zurich. He showed great talent for research as a young man and worked as assistant to the celebrated Professor Kundt before becoming a teacher. By 1875 he had something of a reputation and was made professor of physics and mathematics at the Agricultural Academy of Hohenheim. He taught also at Strassburg and Giessen before settling down at the University of Würzberg, where he made his most famous discovery.

One day in 1895 he was passing an electric current through a glass tube completely covered by black paper and almost completely drained of air. Although no light from the electric current could be seen because of the black paper, Roentgen noticed that the discharge caused nearby crystals of barium platinocyanide to brighten vividly. He tried placing various objects between the tube and a card on which the same crystals were spread, and found that the objects cast shadows on the card. More experiments proved that the radiation would pass through substances that stopped ordinary light.

Announcement of Roentgen's discovery brought immediate recognition of its value to medicine, and one of the first trials, in the United States, resulted in locating a bullet in a patient's leg. Other scientists began experimenting with Roentgen or X-rays and the Englishman, Sir Herbert Jackson, soon perfected a "focus" tube like the standard X-ray tube of today, far more efficient than the one Roentgen used.

The German physicist has much other valuable research to his credit, in such varied and obscure fields as capillarity, elasticity, piezo-electricity and electro-magnetic rotation of polarized light. The many honors he received included the Nobel prize for physics in 1901 and the Rumford Medal of the Royal Society in 1896. He died at Munich, Feb. 10, 1923.

"The Sultan of Swat"

GEORGE HERMAN

(BABE)

RUTH

DURING THE 1920's, America's fabulous "Golden Age of Sports," when every sport seemed to have record-breakers and fascinating characters, the most incredible figure of all was "Babe" Ruth, the celebrated "Sultan of Swat." He was born at Baltimore in 1895, of a very poor family, and learned baseball at St. Mary's Industrial School. His first professional job was with the Baltimore Orioles, in 1913. The next year he shifted to the Boston Red Sox and began to build the record that still has experts gasping. In his later years as an outfielder and home-run hitter, fans tended to forget what a magnificent pitcher he had been. To mention only one of his many feats on the mound — he pitched and won the longest game in World Series history (1916).

Traded to the New York Yankees for an unprecedented sum, Ruth in 1920 switched to the outfield, so that his bat would be useful every day, and started the most memorable part of his career. "Murderers' Row" would have been a formidable group of hitters without him. With him, it made the Yankees the most famous and profitable ball club in history. Ruth's annual total of home runs grew swiftly till it reached the fantastic peak of sixty for a single season. Sometimes his great teammate, Lou Gehrig, gave him close competition for the lead in circuit hits, and the race between them made wonderful publicity stories, but in his prime no one was the equal of George Herman. Best remembered of the countless stories of his hitting was his "called shot," when -- for the benefit of heckling spectators — he pointed to the center field fence and blasted the next pitch out of the park exactly where he had pointed.

Undisciplined and a mighty eater and drinker, Ruth was often in trouble with his superiors, and when he began to slip in the mid-Thirties the manager's job he wanted was not forthcoming. A decade later he contracted cancer of the throat and after a long illness died in August of 1948. Thousands of Americans sent messages of condolence, from the President down. The massive torso on those spindling legs, the huge, contagious grin and his great love of life had made him an unforgettable and universally beloved figure.

World's Foremost Playwright

WILLIAM
SHAKESPEARE

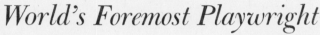

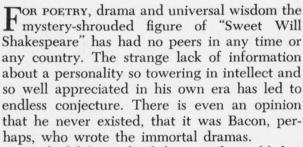

For poetry, drama and universal wisdom the mystery-shrouded figure of "Sweet Will Shakespeare" has had no peers in any time or any country. The strange lack of information about a personality so towering in intellect and so well appreciated in his own era has led to endless conjecture. There is even an opinion that he never existed, that it was Bacon, perhaps, who wrote the immortal dramas.

But faithful search of the records establishes a few things: his birth at Stratford-on-Avon about April 23, 1564; his marriage at the age of eighteen to Anne Hathaway; the births of his three children; his death on his own birthday in 1616; and his will. The rest, except for the plays and the poetry, is probability or surmise.

He probably went briefly to the Stratford free grammar school for his only formal education, and might have been apprenticed to a butcher. He seems to have got into trouble for poaching on the estate of Sir Thomas Lucy, and this may have been the reason for his going to London. What he did there first, no one has an idea. But in 1592 a jealous tirade by his colleague, Robert Greene, placed him in the theatre as an actor and playwright. And by 1594 he was a leading member of a company that played before Elizabeth's court. But he had little acting ability.

His genius, of course, was for the play itself. For a dozen years or more he was chief dramatist of his company, overhauling old manuscripts that were public property and injecting into them the penetrating characterization, the incredible wisdom and the beautiful language which were so peculiarly his.

Shakespeare's non-dramatic poetry, such as *Venus and Adonis* and *The Rape of Lucrece*, has as much power and imagery as the plays. And his famous sonnets are not only gems in themselves, but of particular interest for the hints they contain of happenings in his own life.

From casual comments of Ben Johnson and his other intimates, it appears that Shakespeare was an honorable, tolerant and genial man, who enjoyed company in a tavern and did not take himself too seriously.

FRANZ PETER

SCHUBERT

During his thirty-one years on earth, Schubert composed at least 600 songs, besides many masterpieces of instrumental music, but none of his seventeen operas won lasting acceptance and, except for a very moderate success beginning three years before his death, he lived always in poverty.

Son of a schoolmaster, he was born at Vienna, Jan. 31, 1797. His father placed him in the court chapel's chorister's school at the age of eleven. During his five years there he spent much of his time at musical composition, and when he left, in 1813, to instruct in his father's school, he continued to compose as a relief from the boredom of teaching. By 1817, when he was twenty, some of his best work was behind him.

A popular baritone named Vogl introduced Schubert's songs to his native city of Vienna and helped him acquire some reputation. Two of his comic operas were produced in 1820, with songs that gained wide popularity, but there was little income for the composer. He had no business instinct, so his friends divided the task

of seeing to his support, one finding him a room, another food and so on. In association they arranged musicales for his benefit, which came to be known as "*Schubertiaden.*" Not until after Vogl had sung *Erlkönig* in early 1821 would any publisher touch his songs, and then the arrangement stopped after seven pieces were issued, and Schubert received almost nothing.

For the next three years he strove for stage presentations with discouraging response, though some of this music was as charming as anything he ever wrote. In 1824 he composed his famous octet, *A Sketch for a Grand Symphony* and several other major works, while entertaining a vain passion, according to some biographers, for the Countess Caroline Esterházy.

The following year, after *Mass in A Flat* and the *Unfinished Symphony*, a little prosperity arrived. In 1826 he asked to be made conductor of the Vienna opera, but was turned down for refusing to change one of his songs. Two years later he gave the only concert of his own works. He died Nov. 19 of the same year.

His Questions
Brought Wisdom

SOCRATES

THIS insatiably inquisitive philosopher, devoted to asking and answering questions, never put anything down on paper by which we can judge him. Our knowledge of him comes mostly from two of his disciples, Xenophon, the general who wrote the celebrated *Anabasis,* and Plato who wrote the philosophical dialogues, in which he quoted Socrates but not himself. Probably Xenophon had a military prejudice against a pure intellectual, though Socrates had served with great distinction as an Athenian soldier. And perhaps Plato put words of his own in the older philosopher's mouth.

At any rate, the famous thinker was born in Athens about the year 469 B.C., with a sculptor for a father and a midwife for a mother. They were well enough off to give him a good education in geometry, astronomy, music and gymnastics, the usual Greek subjects. Sophist philosophers, of whom there were many in Athens during his youth, also added to Socrates's knowledge, since he made a point of mingling with them and tirelessly asking the questions for which he later became so famous.

During his military service Socrates proved not only exceptionally brave, but peculiarly indifferent to weather and fatigue. Later as a revered philosopher, he still spurned the comforts of life, wearing only one garment and eating the simplest food. According to Xenophon, he bore with a shrewish wife, Xanthippe, as a means of self-discipline. According to all his friends, he was himself extremely ugly.

His aim in life was to spread knowledge, his belief that only from this could come ethical conduct. His formula was: "Virtue is knowledge; vice is ignorance." His method was conversation—question, answer and discussion, over and over again till every possibility was explored.

In 399 B.C. the Athenians tried Socrates for neglecting the old gods, introducing new ones and corrupting the morals of youth. By a few votes he was declared guilty and ordered to drink poison hemlock. Characteristically, he spent his last day talking with his friends, and in the evening calmly drained the cup.

*Most Independent
Man on Earth*

GEORGE BERNARD
SHAW

As a playwright and critic Shaw has incontestable genius, but it would take more than that to explain the Olympian position he built for himself in the English-speaking world. The briefest visit of an American pilgrim to his home is worth an essay in some magazine; his slightest words get privileged space in newspapers. There is a fascination about his personality—perhaps because of its unpredictability—that is unique.

It took time for him to reach eminence. Born of impoverished Irish "gentry" at Dublin, July 26, 1856, he learned appreciation of music and the drama from his mother. Deciding on a literary career at the age of twenty, he went to London and for nine years lived in poverty, earning exactly six pounds from his work in all that time. Between 1879 and 1883 he wrote five novels, but they were not published till later, and then in a Socialist magazine. A speech by Henry George converted him to the Single Tax, but before acting on his new belief he read Karl Marx's *Capital* and was reconverted to Socialism, in 1884 joining the Fabian Society.

Then he became book critic for the *Pall Mall Magazine,* as well as art critic for the *World* and a little later dramatic critic for the *Saturday Review.* His Fabian speeches also were popular, and now the future had a brighter hue. Between 1891 and 1898 he wrote four plays, with long controversial prefaces, and though none of his dramatic work was staged in London before 1904, he was well established by the mid-90's as a brilliant journalist and debater. In America, however, Richard Mansfield introduced his play, *Arms and the Man,* as early as 1898, following it with *The Devil's Disciple,* and he was accepted in Germany about the same time. His first London success was *John Bull's Other Island,* a satire about Irish character, and it promptly made him a dramatist of note. Some of his other more famous plays are *Mrs. Warren's Profession, Major Barbara* and *The Doctor's Dilemma.* The three regarded as his best, written after the age of sixty, are *Saint Joan, Heartbreak House* and *Back to Methuselah.*

A vegetarian as well as a socialist, Shaw yet has always refused to bind himself to any set way of thinking. His caustic, extravagant, utterly outspoken opinions are peculiarly his own, and perhaps that is what makes him so fascinating.

Tusitala, "Teller of Tales"

ROBERT LOUIS
STEVENSON

No WRITER of adventure stories has ever been more beloved than Robert Louis Stevenson. *Treasure Island* and *Kidnapped* are enduring classics, read by everyone. His poems, collected in such volumes as *A Child's Garden of Verse* and *Ballads*, are equally popular, and *The Strange Case of Dr. Jekyll and Mr. Hyde* stands with Mrs. Shelley's *Frankenstein* as the finest and most blood-curdling of horror stories.

The son of an engineer and builder of lighthouses, Stevenson was born in Scotland, Nov. 13, 1850, and educated at Edinburgh University for the same profession as his father. Shifting his interest to law, he was admitted to the bar in 1875, but a greater leaning toward literature and a lung weakness that kept him searching for healthier climates soon led to his desertion of the legal profession.

An Inland Voyage and *Travels with a Donkey* were his first books, accounts of journeys in France. His first great, and probably most enduring, success was *Treasure Island*, that wonderful romance of pirates and hidden gold. *Prince Otto* appeared in 1885, then *Kidnapped*, *The Black Arrow*, *The Master of Ballantrae* and many other fine tales.

In 1879 Stevenson made his first visit to the United States, because of the illness in San Francisco of Mrs. Fanny Osbourne, whom he had met three years earlier. Without much money, he took steerage passage across the Atlantic and had a hard transcontinental trip, both of which ruined his already weak health. He and Mrs. Osbourne married in 1880 and traveled a great deal in search of a place where he could be well, finally (1890) settling on the Pacific Island of Samoa, where he died Dec. 3, 1894 — but not before even the Samoan natives gave him the appropriate name, Tusitala, "teller of tales."

Stevenson had a special personal charm, a fine courage that dominated his physical weakness, great gifts as a conversationalist and a persistent gaiety that made for him warm friends among the great literary figures of his time. A graceful and witty letter-writer, he had a wide correspondence that, in published form, constitute some of his pleasantest work

*Her Novel Helped Start
the Civil War*

HARRIET BEECHER
STOWE

Timing has much to do with the success of any book, and whatever literary merit *Uncle Tom's Cabin* has or has not, it was timed perfectly, in the spring of 1852, when the great intersectional struggle over slavery was warming up for the hot words that preceded the war.

Its author, Harriet Beecher Stowe, was born June 14, 1811, at Litchfield, Conn., daughter of the articulate Rev. Lyman Beecher and sister of the equally erudite and oratorical Henry Ward Beecher. In 1832 she moved with her father and elder sister, Catherine, to Cincinnati, Ohio, where she took active part in establishing a pioneer college for women. Harriet compiled a school geography, wrote stories and sketches for the local newspapers, and gave encouragement to the literary life of the community. In 1836 she married Calvin Ellis Stowe, an abolitionist minister, who no doubt helped to confirm her antipathy to slavery, already formed by fugitive slaves in Cincinnati and visits in the South.

In 1850 her husband was made a professor at Bowdoin College in Maine, and on moving there she began to write *Uncle Tom's Cabin or Life Among the Lowly.* First published serially in an abolitionist periodical, it appeared in book form, March, 1852, and immediately found an enormous audience, eventually being translated into twenty-three languages. In reply to criticism, she shortly afterwards wrote *A Key to Uncle Tom's Cabin*, quoting evidence of the charges she made in the original book. In 1853 she went to England, hoping to forge a bond between English and American women on the question of slavery. In 1856 she published another fictional tract called *Dred; A Tale of the Dismal Swamp*, proving the necessary deterioration of any society that tolerated slavery.

She wrote other novels, stories, sketches, essays on social life and religious poems. After the founding of the *Atlantic Monthly* in 1857 she was a regular contributor to its pages, as well as to the *Independent* and *Christian Union.*

Her husband died in 1886 and she spent the next ten years in seclusion at Hartford, Conn., till her own death, July 1, 1896.

Colossus among Conductors

ARTURO
TOSCANINI

WHEN TOSCANINI made his New York début as a conductor, Nov. 16, 1908, the phrase "unique genius," attached itself securely to his name before the curtain dropped. Not altogether a stranger to criticism in the subsequent forty-odd years, he nevertheless maintained his reputation as a peerless orchestral leader.

He was born March 25, 1867, at Parma, Italy, son of a tailor. He had no family musical background and no family means for musical training, but in Parma of that time any boy of talent could get ahead. He began as a cellist and in his teens toured South America with the opera company of Claudi Rossi. In Rio de Janeiro on June 15, 1886, before his twentieth birthday, Rossi's director resigned abruptly and Toscanini took over. There was great praise for his conducting and from then on it remained his vocation, but years later Toscanini remembered the night chiefly for two minor mistakes he made—a significant indication of his memory for music.

From 1898 to 1907 he conducted at the famous opera center, La Scala at Milan, Italy. In 1908 he came to the Metropolitan Opera in New York with Gatti-Casazza and went on augmenting his enormous reputation as the years passed.

After 1929 he turned from the more strenuous task of conducting opera to symphonic work.

Toscanini's amazing memory early digested the scores of all standard operas and symphonies, including obscure publishers' misprints, and his infallible ear became as feared at rehearsals as his temper. An uncompromising perfectionist, he demanded not only the exact music the composer wrote—through every violin in the orchestra—but the very conception in the composer's mind, even if he never succeeded in getting it down on paper. "Magical performances" were the result and Stokowski called Toscanini the "supreme master of all conductors." But the wear and tear of playing up to his standards sometimes left orchestras, after his departure, unable to play up even to their own standards for long periods.

In 1937 he organized and became conductor of the National Broadcasting Company symphony orchestra and in 1943 surprised some of his more conventional followers by performing George Gershwin's *Rhapsody in Blue*.

[141]

Ill-starred Musical Genius of Russia

PETER ILYITCH
TCHAIKOVSKY

Tchaikovsky's marvelous music was often as badly received as his love for women. When the opera singer, Désirée Artôt, rejected his suit and married another man, he wrote two operas, a symphony and a concerto to ease his sorrow, but the critics were as apathetic as Désirée.

Son of a mining engineer, Peter Ilyitch Tchaikovsky was born May 7, 1840, at Votkinsk, in the province of Viatka. His original aim was to be a lawyer, and he went to law school and worked in the ministry of justice before music took over his life. At the Conservatory of St. Petersburg he studied under Zaremba and received encouragement from Anton Rubinstein, the director of the school, though his musical gifts were less appreciated by Anton than by his brother Nicholas, who, in 1866, invited him to be first head of the Moscow Conservatory.

At Moscow the composer wrote his first opera, *The Chieftain.* Produced in 1869, it was a failure. Tchaikovsky met Rimsky-Korsakov and other "advanced" Russian composers in Moscow, but rejected their musical theories. He also met Désirée Artôt and fell violently in love with her,

but she rejected him. The piano concerto that he wrote in his period of recovery from the blow of her marriage to another man was condemned at first by Nicholas Rubinstein, then Hans von Bülow performed it and Rubinstein reversed his opinion, adding the work to his repertoire.

In 1876 Tchaikovsky met a wealthy widow named Mme. Nadezhda Filaretovna von Meck, who subsequently solved his economic problems by giving him an annual allowance of $3,000. In 1879 his most popular opera, *Eugen Onegin,* was produced and by 1890 he no longer needed Mme. von Meck's generous aid. That same year he married Antonina Ivanovna Milyukova. The alliance lasted only three months, Tchaikovsky's eccentric temperament proving unendurable to his wife. Its failure accentuated his already pronounced morbidness and it required a trip abroad to restore his will to write again.

During the next five years he composed many of his most famous works—the celebrated *Fifth Symphony,* the *1812 Overture,* the opera *Maid of Orleans, The Lake of Swans* ballet, *The Sleeping Beauty* and *Cassenoisette.* What he considered his finest work, the *Pathetic* symphony, was produced in 1893 and won the usual lukewarm reception. He died of cholera, Nov. 6, 1893, before musical opinion reversed itself to acclaim the composition as the finest thing of its kind.

"Fair Deal" President

HARRY S.
TRUMAN

ONE of the greatest political surprises of modern times was the 1948 presidential victory of Mr. Truman over Governor Thomas E. Dewey. Tradition, propaganda and political polls were unanimous in predicting a Republican triumph. The reversal and Mr. Truman's astounding popularity with the American people set off a unique reappraisal of previously accepted methods of judging public opinion.

Central figure in this astonishing upset was one of the least colorful of all American Presidents. Born May 8, 1884, at Lamar, Mo., Harry S. Truman had a high school education, worked on a farm, as a railroad timekeeper and as a bookkeeper. In World War I he served in the Army overseas, rising to a captaincy in the field artillery. Returning, he won the attention of Missouri political boss Tom Pendergast and went through a succession of judgeships to become U. S. Senator in 1934. Just before American entry into World War II he was appointed head of what came to be known as the Truman Committee, investigating expenditures for the defense program. In this position he made a fine reputation as a watchdog of federal funds.

In 1944, when Vice-President Henry Wallace had alienated himself from Democratic leaders, Mr. Roosevelt accepted Truman as his running mate for the fourth term. When F. D. R. died, April 12, 1945, Truman became President. The war went on to its already planned conclusion, but afterwards President Truman ran into trouble, both in foreign and domestic affairs. The great schism with Russia developed swiftly. Labor, restive after the long war years of dutiful quiescence, demanded more consideration. Inflation perturbed the consumer. To most commentators, Truman's measures seemed ineffectual, and by the summer of 1948 his Republican adversary, Governor Dewey, was an overwhelming choice to be the next President.

Blundering in the Republican campaign and an unnoted shift in agricultural sentiment were probably the chief elements that defeated Dewey. But the over-all effect was a national endorsement of Roosevelt's New Deal philosophy, in which Truman had put his faith.

[143]

Supreme War Novelist

COUNT LEO
TOLSTOY

A nna Karenina and War and Peace are required reading in schools and colleges. Their author is required thinking by all literate persons. No writer in any language has more admirably depicted psychological difficulties between men and women or the endless, agonizing tension of war.

Count Leo Nikolaievitch Tolstoy was born Sept. 9, 1828, at Yasnaya Polyana, in the province of Tula, Russia. Member of a wealthy noble family, he had an easy youth, studying at Karzan University (1844-1847), and in 1851 had his first experience of army life, as a gentleman-volunteer serving on the staff of Prince Gortschakoff in Turkey. He later fought in the Crimean War and took an active part in the storming of Sevastopol in 1855. During these four years he wrote and published several novels and poems, the first story being *Childhood,* and earned a modest literary reputation. But it was the three sketches he wrote about Sevastopol, with their strikingly realistic reporting of war horror, that established him as a top-rank writer.

After the war Tolstoy resigned from the army and for a while lived the gay literary-social life of contemporary St. Petersburg. Then he travled in Italy and Germany and, becoming more conscious of social inequalities, wrote as a protest *The Memoirs of Prince Mekhlyudov.*

In 1862 he married the eighteen-year-old Sophie Behrs, who undoubtedly provided material for his most successful novel, the tragic story of an unhappy marriage, *Anna Karenina,* published in the years 1875 and 1876. Ten years earlier came his magnificent account of the Napoleonic campaign in Russia, *War and Peace,* which made secure his fame as one of the world's greatest novelists.

As he grew older Tolstoy became more and more conscious of his responsibility to the overburdened peasantry of his country, going so far as to restrict his dress, diet and manner of life to their level. He also turned against many of the beliefs of the Orthodox Church and gradually evolved his own form of Christianity, based on the Gospels and emphasizing poverty, humility and non-resistance as the highest virtues. His creed is called "Tolstoyism."

In his later years he wrote very little fiction, but gave his brilliant mind to essays on social, religious and philosophical subjects. He died of pneumonia in a railroad station, Nov. 20, 1910.

Prince of Scoffers

VOLTAIRE

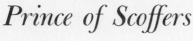

THIS great 18th Century French satirist lived almost as stormy a life as his celebrated character, Candide. His brilliantly witty ridicule of important people brought him to prison and exile on more than one occasion, and the influential friends he made with his sharp tongue and pen he usually lost by the same means.

François Marie Arouet was his real name and he was born in Paris Nov. 21, 1694, and educated at a Jesuit college. His first attention as a writer came when he submitted a poem in the Academy contest, failed to win the prize, then wrote a lampoon about his successful rival. This and some other poems earned him a minor reputation as a wit in his early twenties. After a brief exile and eleven months in the Bastille for insulting the Regent, he presented his first tragedy, *Oedipe,* in 1718, and became a real success. This was when he took the name Voltaire.

In 1723 he published an epic poem about Henry IV, in which he advocated religious liberalism too vigorously for the authorities to permit its distribution in France. Three years later he was back in the Bastille, after a quarrel with the Chevalier de Rohan-Chabot, and then was banished for two years to England.

Returning to Paris about 1728, Voltaire made a considerable fortune by shrewd speculation, but continued to write. His *Letters Concerning the English Nation* made a great stir, informing his previously unaware countrymen about free institutions across the Channel. The fifteen years from 1734 to 1749, most of which he spent at the chateau of his intimate friend Mme. du Châtelet, were extremely productive: essays, stories, dramas, poems, novels, satires flowed from his pen. After her death he visited Frederick the Great, who had invited him to live at the Prussian court in Berlin. Their strong personalities soon clashed, however, and Voltaire went back to France. He died May 30, 1778, from the excitement and fatigue of attending the successful opening of his tragedy, *Irene.*

Candide, published in 1759, is Voltaire's most familiar work for readers of English.

His Fiction came True

JULES
VERNE

Jules Verne not only deserves high credit for creating an entirely new kind of fiction story, involving expeditions into the future, he also wins startled applause for the accuracy of so many of his predictions. As Marshall Lyautey said, "the advance of the peoples is merely living the novels of Jules Verne."

Born at Nantes Feb. 8, 1828, he studied law in Paris, but though he practiced this profession, he also had a deep interest in the theatre and, as early as 1848, collaborated with Michel Carré on two operettas. Two years later he had a comedy in verse produced, and in this Alexandre Dumas the younger had some share of the writing. Then some fanciful stories of travel he wrote for a magazine brought him realization of his true bent.

Five Weeks in a Balloon, published in 1862, was his first considerable success in the new field. And for the next quarter of a century scarcely a year passed without some astounding tale of future scientific discoveries and mechan-

ical inventions—most of which, from the submarine on up, have been made and put to practical use since publication of his stories. The best known of his works include *Voyage to the Middle of the Earth* (1864), *From the Earth to the Moon* (1865), *Twenty Thousand Leagues Under the Sea* (1869) and the *Trip Around the World in Eighty Days* (1872). Adaptation of this last story to the theatre and of another excellent adventure tale called *Michael Strogoff* proved to be Verne's most successful experiences with stage drama.

Although he never became a member of the French Academy, several of his stories won its acclaim and he did become a member of the Legion of Honor. But the true measure of his genius is the delight with which his books have been read by millions in many languages. Their bright and lively style—partly an inheritance from Dumas—the subordination of romantic entanglements in his plots, and the fact that they are essentially dream stories that come true have made them universally fascinating, but a particular treasure for young readers. Verne died March 24, 1905.

The Longest Reign in British History

QUEEN

VICTORIA

MANY things that were neither very moral nor very orderly happened during the sixty-three years Victoria spent on the English throne, but the Victorian Era now has a nostalgic aura of contentment, prosperity and well directed progress that is due in no little part to the remarkable qualities of the Hanoverian Queen who gave it her name.

Almost from infancy (she was born May 24, 1819) she had the theory and practice of proper government dinned into her little head, so that few eighteen-year-olds (or older heads, for that matter) could have been better prepared for the coronation that made her Queen in 1838. Two years later she married Albert, Prince of Saxe-Coburg, who turned out to be an equally admirable character. Together (till his death in 1861) they enjoyed a wonderful success as rulers, and their simple, unostentatious manner of living and obvious self-discipline were a unique example to their subjects.

Victoria's was an eventful reign, and she took an active, if strictly constitutional, part in most of its events. Extension of the franchise, for example (1865-1868), owed a good deal to her

efforts with Lord Derby. Disraeli acquired the Suez Canal for Britain and made Victoria Empress of India. There was fighting—the Opium War in China (1840-1842), the Crimean War (1854-1856), the Indian Mutiny (1857-1858), the Transvaal War (1880) and others. British domination was established in Egypt and the status of Canada and Australia within the Empire regularized. Through all these happenings Victoria worked tirelessly for harmony between the home government and its dependencies. The sixtieth year of her reign (1897), was celebrated as a Diamond Jubilee throughout the Empire, with lavish pageantry.

Victoria died Jan. 22, 1901, and was universally mourned. The casket containing her body was carried from the Isle of Wight between twin rows of warships and accompanied by a military procession from Windsor to London.

Laurence Housman's play, *Victoria Regina*, delightfully presented the Queen and her Consort to Americans a few years ago, with Helen Hayes memorably cast as Victoria.

Renaissance Artist who
Tried to Build an Airplane
LEONARDO DA
VINCI

Leonardo is almost as famous for his versatility as for his painting. Not content with his unsurpassed mastery of the brush, he made a name for himself in sculpture, music, writing, engineering, architecture and scientific research. He even worked to devise a flying machine.

The illegitimate son of a wealthy notary, Leonardo was born in 1452 at the town of Vinci near Florence. In the latter city, then the intellectual center of Europe, his father provided him with the best education obtainable, and about 1470 he became a pupil-apprentice of the famous sculptor and painter, Andrea del Verrocchio. His own work, however, shows little trace of outside artistic influence, being largely the product of his acute power of observation.

About 1483 he moved to Milan, attaching himself to the court of Duke Locovico Sforza, for whom he directed pageants, set up a system of hydraulic irrigation for his lands and conducted other business, besides painting. Here in 1498, on the walls of the monastery of Santa Maria delle Grazie, he painted the celebrated *Last Supper*. Damp walls and an unsuitable

choice of paint soon caused deterioration, but through centuries of necessary restorations it has remained one of Leonardo's best appreciated works. Unluckily, most of the paintings of his Milan period have been lost.

In 1502 he went into the service of Caesar Borgia as an engineer and architect, traveling over most parts of Italy. After his return to Florence he spent four years painting the *Mona Lisa*, his and probably history's most famous canvas. Even at the end of the four years he considered it unfinished. In 1506 he became court painter to Louis XII of France and he spent his last years in that country, dying May 2, 1519.

The Virgin of the Rocks, St. John the Baptist and *Saint Anne* are among the lamentably few Leonardo paintings that have survived to us. His *Mona Lisa* was the cause of a sensation in 1911 when it disappeared from the Louvre in Paris. Two years later an Italian who claimed patriotic motives for the theft, was discovered with the painting. Before its return to the Louvre the masterpiece was viewed by multitudes in various Italian cities.

Master
of the Music Drama

RICHARD
WAGNER

Somewhat precocious in literature—he had translated twelve books of the *Odyssey* when he was thirteen and written a tragedy the following year—Wagner waited long, bitter years for appreciation of his music, still longer for a favorable reception of his true life work, the music drama, now so familiar to opera-goers.

He was born at Leipzig, May 22, 1813, and educated in Dresden. His first operatic composition, *Die Feen*, was begun when he was twenty, though not performed till five years after his death. After varied musical activities in Konigsberg, Heidelberg and Riga, he tried Paris, where three years of effort failed to get his opera, *Rienzi*, produced. On his return to Dresden, however, the opera was performed, and with great success, the result being his appointment as *kapellmeister*. But his next two operas, *Der Fliegende Hollander* and *Tannhauser*, were failures. To set the public straight, he wrote several essays explaining his then unorthodox theory that book, music, acting and stage setting are of nearly equal value in obtaining operatic effects.

In 1848 the Hungarian composer, Liszt, gave a more successful presentation of *Tannhauser* at Weimar and the two musicians became fast friends, Wagner's second marriage being to Liszt's daughter. He then completed *Lohengrin*, but before it could be staged he went into a twelve-year political exile, a period of great hardship. During it he worked on the *Nibelungen Ring* and *Tristan und Isolde*, the latter his first opera to be performed (1865) after the exile ended. It also marked the beginning of the good fortune he was to enjoy for the rest of his life. His light opera, *Die Meistersinger*, was successfully presented three years later.

Although he had finished writing the poem in 1852, Wagner did not complete his great *Nibelungen* trilogy till 1874. Two years earlier a theatre for the production of his operas had been started at Bayreuth and when work ended in 1876 the *Nibelungen Ring* was there presented. After his death, Feb. 13, 1883, his wife Cosima found support to continue the annual Wagnerian festivals at Bayreuth.

[149]

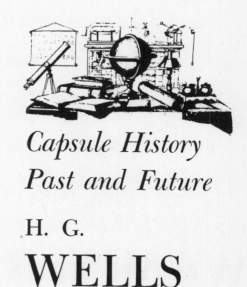

Capsule History
Past and Future

H. G.
WELLS

Best known and perhaps most original of Wells' varied and voluminous contributions to English literature is his two-volume *Outline of History*, in which he by-passed the dry-as-dust methods of conventional historians to produce a wonderfully readable and concise account of everything that has happened to the world. But the list of his titles includes books of many other kinds—fantastic science novels, like *The Time Machine;* fiction aimed at social reform, such as *Ann Veronica,* a story that espoused the cause of feminine emancipation; novels of contemporary English life, such as *Mr. Britling Sees It Through,* a widely popular book during World War I; novels of discussion, like *Mr. Blettsworthy on Rampole Island;* and simple stories of character and humor, like *Love and Mr. Lewisham.* His prodigious energy produced far too many books to itemize, and he wrote industriously for magazines and newspapers as well.

The store his father owned made so little money that Wells Senior had to play professional cricket to keep the family going. Born at Kent Sept. 21, 1866, young Wells was apprenticed to a linen draper, but could endure the trade for only two years. By winning scholarships he managed to attend the Royal College of Science and London University, studying biology under the famous Professor Huxley. Then he had a period of teaching biology himself. At the same time he began to contribute articles to periodicals and in 1893 decided to devote himself entirely to writing.

The Time Machine appeared in 1895. Although its fanciful scientific flavor had a resemblance to Jules Verne, Wells was so much more interested in social and economic affairs that his excursion into the future had a quite different quality from the Frenchman's. Another such fantasy was published in 1898, *War of the Worlds.* It described an invasion of the Earth by inhabitants of Mars. Presentation over the radio many years later caused sensational confusion and riots when North and South American listeners, on separate occasions, mistook fiction for fact and thought a real Martian attack was taking place. Wells died Aug. 13, 1946.

"First in the Hearts
of His Countrymen"

GEORGE

WASHINGTON

Parson Weems' exaggerations have succeeded in dehumanizing this great man to an amazing extent. His genius as a military leader and statesman is recognized and applauded, but what sticks in most minds is the preposterous story of the cherry tree, and the first President of the United States comes down to us as a cold, inhuman, improbable figure. Considering the love his contemporaries bore him, one has trouble believing this picture.

His father, Augustine Washington, left six Virginia plantations, near Fredericksburg, to George, who came into the property in 1752, when he was twenty. Tobacco-raising, taking care of stock, surveying, and his duties as a supervisor occupied more of his time than schooling. During the French and Indian War he served with the Virginia troops, rising to be commander of the Virginia militia, and in 1758 led the advance guard that took Ft. Duquesne (Pittsburgh). Marriage the following year with wealthy Martha Custis made Washington one of the richest tobacco men in Virginia.

From the beginning he was active in the Revolutionary cause and he became commander of the Colonial armies soon after fighting began. Victories like Trenton and Princeton, setbacks like New York and Monmouth, troubles with Congress, lack of food and money for his army, treachery on the part of subordinates and public weariness with a protracted war, all were grist to the mill of Washington's determination to win through to independence. With much-needed French aid and his own redoubtable military skill he finally forced the surrender of Cornwallis at Yorktown in October of 1781.

Two terms as President, beginning in April, 1790, established him as a statesman of the first order. Rejecting the title of king, he firmly set the course of the new republic, urging a strong national government, neutrality in foreign affairs, unified finances. Refusing a third term nomination, he retired in 1797 to his Mt. Vernon estate and died there two years later, on Dec. 14.

20th Century Moses

CHAIM

WEIZMANN

Fɪʀsᴛ ᴘʀᴇsɪᴅᴇɴᴛ of Israel, the world's newest nation, Dr. Chaim Weizmann is a rare combination of statesman and scientist, of abstract thinker and practical worker, of political zealot and educator. As a long-time leader of World Zionism and the individual whose efforts opened the way to establishment of a national home for the Jews, it is peculiarly appropriate that he should have been named (in May, 1948) first head of the independent Hebrew state.

Born Nov. 27, 1875, near Pinsk in Russia, he early learned the effects of anti-Semitism, being barred from schools in Russia and forced to take his scientific training in Germany. At Berlin and Freiberg he immersed himself not only in chemistry, but also in the newly organized Zionist movement. After lecturing at Geneva he moved (about 1904) to England and taught biochemistry at the University of Manchester, later becoming a British subject. Active in Zionist circles, he conceived the idea of a Hebrew university in Palestine during these years.

As director of the Admiralty laboratories in World War I, he discovered a desperately needed synthetic acetone for use in manufacturing the smokeless powder called cordite. His reward was the Balfour Declaration (1917), which opened the doors for Jewish settlement in Palestine. The next year, while fighting still continued not many miles away, he laid the cornerstone of his university at Jerusalem.

In a barren and almost unpopulated country, which Palestine then was, a great university seemed bizarre. But Weizmann believed that a center for research and education was a prerequisite for a successful Jewish state. In considerable degree the flowering of agriculture and industry that developed in Palestine over the next thirty years stemmed from his idea. Chemical and agricultural research done at the university made possible the sustaining of a whole new population.

Dr. Weizmann steered his little homeland through treacherous political currents for many years before winning international recognition of its independence. At the same time he made a wide variety of important contributions to science and technology, including dyes, synthetic fuel, synthetic rubber and cheap synthetic food.

[152]

"Liberty and Union, Now and Forever"

DANIEL WEBSTER

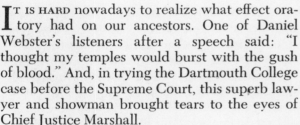

I**T IS HARD** nowadays to realize what effect oratory had on our ancestors. One of Daniel Webster's listeners after a speech said: "I thought my temples would burst with the gush of blood." And, in trying the Dartmouth College case before the Supreme Court, this superb lawyer and showman brought tears to the eyes of Chief Justice Marshall.

A New Hampshire farm boy, born at Salisbury, Jan. 18, 1782, Webster was educated at Phillips Exeter and Dartmouth at very real sacrifice to his family. Balancing a lifelong fondness for hunting and fishing, his passionate love of reading not only made him a brilliant scholar, but also provided him with an inexhaustible fund of quotation for both his public speeches and his arguments in court. After studying law in a Boston office, he was admitted to the Massachusetts bar in 1805 and soon became a leading attorney at Portsmouth.

His political career, which began with election to Congress in 1813, was a mixture of brilliance and frustration. His eloquence made him a senator and eventually Secretary of State (under Harrison, Tyler and Fillmore), but his am-

bition to be elected President never was realized. Probably his most important act historically was to side with Henry Clay in the Missouri Compromise on slavery, which delayed the Civil War by ten years and permitted the North to grow strong enough to win the conflict, though at the time Northern abolitionists abused him for his stand. As a diplomat he made a peaceful settlement of the northern boundary dispute with Great Britain. It was in the complex field of public finance, however, that his talents best displayed themselves, and many of his progressive ideas were later incorporated in the Federal Reserve System. This despite a complete inability to keep his personal accounts in order.

Webster's law practice brought him a large income, but his careless financial habits, combined with heavy drinking and extravagance, made him a good deal of private trouble.

On his deathbed, Oct. 24, 1852, he made a long speech, then after a rest asked: "Have I, on this occasion, said anything unworthy of Daniel Webster?" His family, his doctor and gathered friends all said no.

[153]

"The Good Gray Poet"

WALT

WHITMAN

Walt Whitman really wrote only one book, *Leaves of Grass*, but it grew from a slender, 95-page volume on first publication in 1855 till the edition of 1860 had 456 pages and later ones contained still more and newer verses. It grew in another way, too. At first the unrhymed, irregular free verse seemed fantastic to readers accustomed to more conventional poetry, and it was not taken seriously. Then Ralph Waldo Emerson gave Whitman strong public praise and intellectuals began to regard him with the admiration that was his due. Soon he had a wide and responsive audience, not only in the United States but abroad.

The poet, born May 31, 1819, near Huntington, L. I., went briefly to public schools in Brooklyn and New York, but acquired the learning that made him so essentially a true voice of America by voluminous reading and the habit of meeting his fellow men at close quarters. An inveterate wanderer, he took long walking tours through the West, the South, the Southwest and into Canada. His occupations were singularly varied. He worked as a carpenter, typesetter,

doctor's and lawyer's assistant, teacher, newspaper reporter and editor, contractor and real estate salesman, Army nurse during the Civil War, and Federal Government employe in the Interior and Treasury Departments. Through all these experiences he kept an intense interest in the natural conduct of people he met, and glorified that ordinary way of life over the formalized subject matter of traditional poets.

The three years he spent nursing Union Army wounded during the Civil War had a tremendous emotional effect on Whitman. They also broke his health. As a result, in 1865, he was given a post in the Interior Department. A later edition of *Leaves of Grass* contained such outspoken material that offended readers succeeded in having him dismissed. William Douglas O'Connor than wrote a poetical criticism of the affair, called *The Good Gray Poet*, which not only got Whitman another government job, but fastened the sobriquet on him for keeps.

In 1873 he became paralyzed and lived the final eighteen years of his life in Camden, N. J., poor but cheerful and tremendously admired. He died March 27, 1892.

Master Dictionary Maker

NOAH
WEBSTER

Probably no other English dictionary has sold so many copies or had so much influence, at least in the United States, as Webster's. Begun about 1807, it took him twenty years to complete, in the first edition of two volumes, which had 12,000 words listed. A revised and enlarged edition appeared in 1840 and, just a few days before his death, May 28, 1843, he finished an appendix. From this foundation work has stemmed a long series of revisions and abridgements that still appear at regular intervals.

Descended on his father's side from John Webster, governor of Connecticut, and on his mother's side from Governor William Bradford of Plymouth Colony, Noah was born Oct. 16, 1758, at West Hartford, Conn. He graduated from Yale in 1778, taught school for a while, then studied law and was admitted to the Connecticut bar in 1781. Much of his time for the next few years, however, he spent writing the *Grammatical Institute of the English Language*, published in three parts between 1783 and 1785. It was a combination grammar-speller-reader and had enormous success, reaching by 1861 a sale of more than a million copies a year. The *Blue-Backed Speller*, as part of it was called, by 1910 had sold 60,000,000 copies.

Webster also wrote a number of political essays during this period and felt that a group issued in 1785, which he called *Sketches of American Policy*, foreshadowed the U. S. Constitution. After a brief return to teaching, as head of an Episcopal school in Philadelphia, he tried professional journalism in New York, editing the *American Magazine*. It failed after a year, and he practised law in Hartford for five years before starting another New York publication, *The Minerva*.

Connecticut and Massachusetts politics occupied him next. He held various public offices in both States and was one of the founders of Amherst College in Massachusetts. A paramount legislative aim with him, both at this time and earlier, was a uniform copyright law. The year 1824-1825 he spent in England and Paris gathering material for the dictionary, which was first published in 1828. Webster's simplification of spelling and his genius for definition made it an outstanding American reference book.

WOODROW
WILSON

Like other great American Presidents, Woodrow Wilson had his plans for a domestic reform program knocked awry by war. The world conflict of 1914-1918 determined him, however, to widen his aims to cover all the civilized nations. His most ambitious dream was the League of Nations, and he lived to see it established, though his own country profoundly disappointed him by refusing to join.

Wilson's background was unusually religious and scholarly for a modern American President. He was born at Staunton, Va., Dec. 28, 1856, son of a Presbyterian minister, and after graduating from Princeton (1879), went on to study law at the University of Virginia and history and government at Johns Hopkins. Later he taught at Bryn Mawr, Connecticut Wesleyan and Princeton, making a considerable reputation for himself by his writings as an expert in political science. In 1902 he became president of Princeton and at once instituted reforms that caused much controversy at the university.

Wilson's political career began with his election as governor of New Jersey in 1910. Liberal legislation brought him wider fame and in 1912 he received the Democratic Presidential nomination, on the forty-sixth ballot. Theodore Roosevelt's split with Taft weakened the Republicans and Wilson became twenty-eighth President of the United States.

Before German submarine attacks forced the United States into the war, there was time for Wilson to arrange the passing of many progressive laws, among them the Federal income tax, the Federal Reserve, the Federal Trade Commission, the Clayton Anti-Trust act and the Underwood tariff. On the outbreak of World War I (1914) he declared a policy of strict neutrality and tried to mediate among the participants. Later he laid down the celebrated "Fourteen Points" as a basis for the final peace settlement.

He attended the Peace Conference in Paris, receiving great popular acclaim in Europe and achieving the inclusion of his League of Nations plan in the peace treaty. Then the isolationist American Senate refused to join and in the election of 1920 was backed by the people, who returned the Republicans to power. Wilson fell ill campaigning and never wholly recovered, dying in Washington Feb. 3, 1924.

His Gin Made Cotton the Crop of the South

ELI
WHITNEY

Eli Whitney's invention of the cotton gin, a mechanical device to separate the seeds from cotton fiber, was a vitally important development in the American South's concentration on this agricultural product, since it saved an incalculable amount of manual labor. But Whitney himself had so much trouble establishing his rights to the profits from his invention that in disgust he shifted to the manufacture of guns.

A native of Westboro, Mass., he was born Dec. 8, 1765, and counted on his precocious mechanical ability for a good deal of the money that saw him through Yale. After his graduation in 1792 he visited the widow of General Nathaniel Greene, Revolutionary War hero, at her Savannah, Ga., plantation. A number of clever household gadgets he contrived during the stay so impressed Mrs. Greene that she introduced Whitney to plantation owners who had been seeking a machine to separate the short-fiber upland cotton from its seeds.

The young inventor went to work promptly and within a few weeks had built a successful model of the new device. It was a wooden cylinder surrounded by rows of slender spikes which penetrated a grid so fine that the seeds could not pass its mesh, but the lint was pulled out. A revolving brush took the lint from the spikes and the seeds fell into a compartment. Operated by hand, the cotton gin cleaned fifty pounds of lint a day.

Whitney found a partner in Connecticut and set up a factory to manufacture the gins, being granted a patent in 1794. Demand was so great that they could not supply it, and had to enlist the help of country blacksmiths. But in 1796 a patent for a slightly different gin was granted to Hogden Holmes and, though Whitney in 1807 won a clear title to his invention, the interim legal battle was so expensive and troublesome that Whitney shifted to the manufacture of guns. In the end he received license fees from various Southern States, $50,000 from South Carolina, $30,000 from North Carolina, etc.

His firearms factory was notable for early introduction of standardized parts and the division of labor. Whitney died in 1825.

The Man Who Rebuilt London

SIR CHRISTOPHER
WREN

L ONDON's devastating fire of 1666 presented to Sir Christopher Wren an opportunity as remarkable as his own architectural genius. A chance to plan a whole city, as well as to design many of its important buildings, is something other architects dream of, but Wren actually had. And the fact that his complete scheme was never carried out does not detract from its beauty and grandeur.

His talent for designing, curiously enough, did not manifest itself till after he had made a wide reputation as a mathematician and astronomer. Born Oct. 20, 1632, at East Knoyle, Wiltshire, of a prominent Church family, young Wren studied at Oxford and later became professor of astronomy, first at Gresham College, London, then at Oxford. One of his early achievements was to aid in perfecting the barometer. It was not until 1663 that any structure of his design (the chapel at Pembroke College, Cambridge) was actually built. Within the next three years he planned a number of buildings for both Oxford and Cambridge.

Then came the fire. It destroyed so much of London that the authorities decided a master plan of rebuilding was advantageous, and gave Wren the task of drawing it up. Whereas the city previously had been a maze of crooked alleys and overcrowded tenements, his conception called for wide streets radiating sensibly from a central point, large parks, fine waterfront structures and impressive public buildings. Many of these buildings, including the Royal Exchange, Temple Bar, the College of Physicians, Buckingham House, and Marlborough House, were erected from his plans. The new St. Paul's Cathedral, generally considered his masterpiece, was built not only from his design, but under his supervision. Property holders later prevented much of his over-all plan from being carried out, but enough of it survived to make the city far more beautiful than before.

For this work Wren was knighted in 1673 and made president of the Royal Society in 1681. He died Feb. 26, 1723, and was buried under the choir of St. Paul's Cathedral, where a tablet bears an epitaph that is translated: "If you seek his monument, look about you."

Founder of Rhode Island

ROGER
WILLIAMS

Unlike many of his contemporaries, Roger Williams believed the Indians owned America as a birthright and deserved payment for the land on which white invaders settled. He bargained for his own settlement at Providence with Indian chiefs in their own language.

Little is known about his early life, except that he was born in London about 1604 and probably educated at Cambridge, with Sir Edward Coke as his patron. Going on to study theology, he became chaplain in 1629 for a Sir William Macham, of Otes, Essex. Declining advancement in the church, he turned Puritan and in February, 1631, moved with his wife to Boston. He worked for a while in a Salem church, but could not subscribe to the opinions of his superiors and left for the Plymouth Colony, where he spent two years as an assistant pastor and also studied the Indian languages. Returning to Salem in 1633, he again got into trouble through his forthright assertions that civil authorities had no power over an individual's religious life and that the King's patent for land was invalid unless the Indians were paid.

The Massachusetts General Court put him on trial in July, 1635, and when he refused to retract his statements banished him from the colony, threatening to send him back to England to stop the spread of his beliefs in the New World. He then escaped with a few followers and founded Providence. Complete freedom of worship was its basic creed and it quickly attracted persecuted settlers from other areas. Williams's habitual friendship with the Indians in the early days of the colony enabled him to dissuade the Narragansett tribe from joining an attack on Massachusetts.

In Rhode Island Williams set up the first American Baptist Church, but in a short time lost faith in complete immersion, and rejected all creeds except a belief in fundamental Christianity. He twice visited England, in 1643 and 1651, to obtain a clear charter for his colony, and became a friend of Cromwell and the poet Milton. Elected president of Rhode Island in 1654, he died at Providence in March, 1683.

[159]

They Gave Wings to Man

WILBUR AND ORVILLE
WRIGHT

RARELY in history have two brothers been so closely associated with a single great event that their names became inseparable. Although thirty-six years elapsed between the death of Wilbur Wright in 1912 and that of his brother Orville in 1948, their marvelous achievement forever linked the two.

Sons of an editor who later became a bishop of the United Brethren Church, Wilbur and Orville were born, respectively, at Millville, Ind., April 16, 1867, and Dayton, Ohio, Aug. 19, 1871. Lifelong bachelors, they were operating a bicycle business in Dayton when they became interested in the glider experiments of the German pioneer, Otto Lilienthal, and from a hobby soon developed their fascination into a rigorous scientific pursuit. Discovering that much then current information on aerodynamics had no foundation in fact, they gathered their own data on such important matters as lift and drag of airfoils, using a wind tunnel that they built themselves in 1901.

By the next fall they felt they had learned enough to design a workable airplane. Motive power was to be a four-cylinder, twelve h.p.

gasoline engine, and total weight of the machine, including pilot, was to be 750 pounds. In December, 1903, they were ready for tests, and at Kitty Hawk, N. C., the historic first piloted flight, of which mankind had dreamed so long, was successfully completed.

The Wright brothers had flown, but they still needed to learn how to fly. It was nearly two years before they discovered how to avoid slipping into a tail spin from a sharp turn. They also needed financial backing to manufacture the machines, and that required European demonstration of their aeronautical ability. Royalty came to see them fly, there was great excitement, and after returning to America they succeeded in selling a plane to the Government for $30,000, the Army later setting up an aviation school with Orville as instructor. They also organized the Wright Company to make airplanes.

Samuel Langley, head of the Smithsonian Institution, had flown models of powered planes (Nov. 1896) before the Wrights took off at Kitty Hawk, but they were not piloted. Wilbur and Orville were the first pilots of powered planes.